THE
MASTER PLAN
VOLUME 1

Leavitt Peak Press

ISBN: 978-1-969865-11-4 Paperback
ISBN: 978-1-969865-12-1 Ebook

Rev. date: 10/07/2025

THE
MASTER PLAN
VOLUME 1

OSCAR GREEN

I dedicate the first installment of this series on *the Master Plan* to everyone who has ever had the thought there was more to this life than this, the life of our temporal existence.

Many who have been long dead and buried will wake up, some to eternal life, others to eternal shame.

"'Men and women who have lived wisely and well will shine brilliantly, like the cloudless, star-strewn night skies. And those who put others on the right path to life will glow like stars forever.

"'This is a confidential report, Daniel, for your eyes and ears only. Keep it secret. Put the book under lock and key until the end. In the interim there is going to be a lot of frantic running around, trying to figure out what is going on.' (Daniel 12:2-4 MSG).

This has been a work of faith, persistent hope, and a labor of love; I pray the Master is pleased.

Contents

King James Version–Version Information

In 1604, King James I of England authorized that a new translation of the Bible into English be started. It was finished in 1611, just 85 years after the first translation of the New Testament into English appeared (Tyndale, 1526). The Authorized Version, or King James Version, quickly became the standard for English-speaking Protestants. Its flowing language and prose rhythm has had a profound influence on the literature of the past 300 years. The King James Version present on the Bible Gateway matches the 1987 printing. The KJV is public domain in the United States.

Copyright Information–No copyright information available.

The Message

The Living Bible (TLB)

Expanded Translation (ET)

Copyright Information

The NIV text may be quoted in any form (written, visual, electronic or audio), up to and inclusive of five hundred (500) verses without express written permission of the publisher, providing the verses do not amount to a complete book of the Bible nor do the verses quoted account for twenty-five percent (25%) or more of the total text of the work in which they are quoted.

When the NIV is quoted in works that exercise the above fair use clause, notice of copyright must appear on the title or copyright page or opening screen of the work (whichever is appropriate) as follows:

Introduction

BIBLE (BASIC INSTRUCTION BEFORE LEAVING EARTH)

The Bible is the greatest book ever written, it is also the most important and beloved book of all-time and eternity. Its contents are not earthly, Its writings inspired and preserved by a loving heavenly Father, Who presented It to His children as a gift, to help them get to the next stage of the journey. Yet how paradoxical, it seems while "the Bible" in its many versions and translations is the "Best-Selling" book of all-time the entire world having heard of it, and everyone in our society having access to a copy of it. Yet how inexcusable it is there are but a remnant in each generation who have a good understanding of It, or who can clearly and fully explain Its message of "why we believe, what we believe."

It is an eternal book, written to people having the hope of eternity.

In Its pages, God has given humanity an opportunity to mine great treasures of truth, and the privilege of gaining an eternal mind-set. Truth is, man born of the flesh is carnal by nature, and now exists with a temporal mind with no grasp on eternity, although God has planted "the seed, and the wish to live forever" within his heart. [1] For now, we wear a sheath, an outer casing of flesh; we exist on earth in a temporal state, with our souls exposed to shaping and conditioning.

Nevertheless, what is man's life? We live on earth for a brief time, our life *"is but a vapor, here one moment and gone the next."* [2] Because of a conditioned, "temporal mind-set" men think little on eternal things. As a rule, human beings tend to believe in and allow only what we see or think we understand, and this automatically produces conditioned responses in many. However, this is also where we can unlock the power of faith, "a little faith begets more faith." [3] Because many don't believe, or have a real faith relationship with God, the truths found in Scripture are now becoming more obvious, as this present generation rushes headlong to judgment. When you look at the variety and quantity of literature out there, it becomes obvious that many are searching, searching for the one book which will help them understand and make sense of it all. While all they need is a little more faith in, and meditation on the Bible that they already have. There is little in the form of print media that can explain or bring people to understand the scope of "The Bible." For many talk of it as God's Will and God's Word, few see it as "His Plan." I present this book to you with the hope of changing that. You can understand the Bible; you can see and know there is a Comprehensive Plan, and that God has a Purpose for Creation, and for you. You can know why He put you here on the earth. You can know that He has a Plan and Purpose for your life, far greater than anything you can imagine.

The purpose of this work is to encourage those who have come to know "The Master," and who during this lifetime have looked to see His face and their purpose and role in His Plan. Truth is, because of a temporal worldview, many have set *"the Owner's Manual"* aside. Yes, you might say the Bible is "a Manual" given to us in this life, to help us understand how all of this is supposed to work. Unfortunately, many set it aside because they feel it is too complicated, too hard to understand, and besides, they do not have time.

Now, all of these are symptoms of a conditioned (temporal) mind-set. Sadly, far too many believers content themselves with a good sermon once a week or month, while spending the rest of their time trying to figure out how to manage and make their lives work. The truth is, none of us can afford the luxury of not knowing or understanding the Word of God, none of us can afford the luxury of not knowing "the Truth." It is critical that each one of us not only know "the Owner," but also, "the Owner's Manual"—God's Word. As the book of books, the Bible provides us with:

"Basic Instructions Before Leaving Earth."

We can know His Plan through the instruction received from His Word. The Bible gives understandable teachings, and real answers to the *"Why am I here"* question, thus making it possible for everyone *"born again"* to answer the *"What is it that I must do"* question. Armed with the answers to these questions, you can know your salvation is sure, [4] and then wisely begin redeeming the time living purposefully, no matter what the world around you may be doing. Then you can purposefully do His Will and Work, living on purpose, and fulfilling His plan and purpose for your life. [5] Of course, all of this will happen when you come to realize that God has begun a good work in you and is continuing that work. You are "His workmanship, created in Christ Jesus for good works, which God prepared in advance that we should walk in them." [6]

But you still ask, "Why can't people see the Plan?" There is a twofold reason that most people cannot see the Plan. The first being the seed of sin and natural rebellion, which has produced a natural state of disobedience and unbelief in the human heart, thus, yielding the fruit of apathy and indifference to the "Word of Truth." This is the temporal worldview, the natural state of everyone born into the world. Some think, "I know this book (the Bible) is important, *but who can understand it.*" Others say, *"I don't know and don't want to know"* and still others believe, *"there's more than one way, there are many paths that lead to the Truth."* However, the truth is this, if a person is not born again, born of the Spirit of God, the Bible is a book of nonsense! [7]

Now there is a second and more insidious reason, which caused the first state, thus providing the explanation for both it, and the invisible opposition at work against us. It is the "Father of Sin" and the "enemies of our salvation" who conduct this opposition. It has been their work from the beginning to impugn, distract from, and discredit "the Plan and Word of Truth." They encourage man's natural rebellion, blinding the minds of humanity to the truth of our origin, our condition, the purpose for our existence, and our end. All of this is important for us to understand, and explained in detail, in the Word of God. *Those whose eyes are open can see this in the Plan*; therefore, they are in pursuit of the eternal mind-set. They grasp and understand that although we stand opposed on every side, we have the Victory; [8] because we walk by Faith, not by sight, [9] we stand free in the liberty of Christ. [10] They have moved beyond the temporal world-view, having believed they now see the Eternal.

THIS PRESENT CONFLICT

In the world, we see two distinct worldviews, two ideologies clashing and many continuing conflicts, one-side embracing a culture of life, the other a culture of death, one an eternal world view, the other temporal. Amid these conflicts, many watchers and spectators stand, "undecided, in the valley of decision." [11] To those undecided, Joshua would say, "Choose you this day whom you will serve." [12] Elijah would thunder, "How long will you falter between two opinions? If the LORD is God follow Him; but if Baal, follow him."[13] In addition, from John the Baptist they would hear the words, "Repent, for the kingdom of heaven is at hand!" [14]

In these conflicts, we see the faces of those standing behind the principles of good and those standing behind the principles of evil, and in these last days the lines that separate them are becoming clearer. Now we see two conflicting worldviews, each confirming the Scriptures, and revealing opposite ends of spiritual reality. It is as if God were removing the veil to expose these factions, as if, *God were opening the eyes of His children* to see the reality found in His Prophetic Word and the truth about the Promise of Eternal Life.

As we shall see, this conflict had its beginning in events, which took place, "before God created the race of man." Remember this, it is all about *"The Seed."* [15]

History has shown, and time has revealed that by eating the forbidden fruit of "the tree of knowledge of good and evil," [16] Adam and Eve, not only loss dominion of this world to Satan and his principalities and powers, but they also inherited the potential for producing two kinds of children, *"two seed."* Therefore, the race of man consists of two classes, Biblically speaking, *"two seed,"* "the children of good, and the children of evil."

> *The Word of God reveals these two classes, and their patterns are consistent throughout the witness of human history. In the New Testament they are, "the children of God," and "the children of the Devil." For "in this the children of God and the children of the Devil are manifest: whoever does not practice righteousness is not of God, nor is he who does not Love his brother.* [17]

Here we see all who "practice righteousness and loves his brother" are the children of God. The implication being, everyone who does not practice righteousness (lawlessness) and hates his brother," does not belong to God, they are "children of disobedience, the children of the Devil." [18] With that said, there can be no possibility of a real union of closeness, or peace between these two classes. There cannot be any such as popularly called world unity, world peace or "a brotherhood of man" uniting all religious bodies and sects. [19] There can be no such unity among Christians, Jews, Moslems, Buddhists, Unitarians, Secular Humanist, Agnostics, and Atheists, into one new world order, for at the center of this opposition stands "the Truth." [20] This truth, Jesus spoke of when He said, "Do not suppose that I have come to bring peace to the earth. I did not come to bring peace, but a sword. [21]

That "sword" is the sword of division, which separates those in the light, from those in darkness. It separates those who have gained an eternal perspective, from those who cleave to a temporal one, *those whose eyes are open*, from those whose minds Satan, "the god of this age," has blinded. [22]

The Bible is light, it exposes darkness, Christians love it, unbelievers do not understand it, or they despise and hate it.[23] This is because it exposes them. It exposes the children of God and the children of Satan. It exposes right and wrong. It is the most loved and hated book ever written.

Those who want to be right love it, those who do not hate it.

But we are getting ahead of ourselves as we unfold the Plan. Stated again, the whole Plan was in the mind of our God "Before time began," before He began the work of Creation. From this introduction, let us uncover "The Master Plan."

Part 1 -

"The Master Plan"

*And Elisha prayed, and said, "LORD, I pray, open his eyes that he may see."
Then the LORD opened the eyes of the young man, and he saw. (2 Kings 6:17).*

CHAPTER 1

Life: Temporal or Eternal

"What is man that You are mindful of him, the son of earthborn man that You care for him? Yet You made him for a little while lower than God or heavenly beings the angels; You crowned him with glory and honor. You made him to have dominion over the works of Your hands; You have put all things under his feet." [1]

THE MASTER PLAN

Everyone earnestly seeking the truth is on a journey, a mission, to uncover and discover the Truth. For the believer that journey starts with an unction from the Holy Spirit who leads us to seek out the Truth, [2] the Plan of the Almighty from eternity past. You and I are on a journey, with a mission to uncover that Plan. God devised the terms and conditions of His Sovereign Plan for Creation, [3] at some point in eternity past. Then the Plan existed only in the mind of God; He foresaw the Plan before any of His works of Creation. [4] The Plan included everything in Creation: Heaven, Earth, angels, man, spiritual and physical realms, and everything in space and time. Now while there are plans of angels and plans of men, plans thought about, and plans that live on in dreams, there are those who have begun great plans and undertakings, and those who have completed them, with many more having plans, which have never come to fruition. Among the many, one Plan stands alone. "The Master Plan," trumps all other plans, and is by far the greatest one of all, there is none greater.

> "THE MASTER PLAN," TRUMPS ALL OTHER PLANS, IT IS BY FAR THE GREATEST PLAN OF ALL, AND THERE IS NO GREATER PLAN.

Many are the Plans in a man's Heart, but it is the LORD's Purpose that Prevails.[5]

"The Master Plan" is older than both angels and man and still unfolding. God revealed the Plan through His Word. In the Word we find, "the truth about God, and His Will, Plan, and Purposes for Creation." The Word unveils History, Prophecy, the beginnings of Creation, His testing of angels, and His testing of men, the ages, and dispensations of time, eternity, and the administrations of God's purpose—past, present, and future. The goals of the Plan include redeeming and saving man, judging rebels, and restoring God's kingdom. Now any one of these subjects make a study like this, worthy of our utmost attention, and they are all contained in the One Plan that God wanted you and I to know about.

WHAT IS THE PLAN ABOUT?

Still, some will ask, what is the big deal? *"What is this so-called Master Plan about," "Who is it for," and "Why is it so important?* We will try to answer these questions in the pages ahead. There you will see why you and I are in the greatest struggle of all-time, as the groaning continues, with even greater frequency and intensity, as this present Creation labors to give birth to a *"new Creation."*[6] For now, let's just say that an accurate understanding of the unfolding "Master Plan" will help you understand why you're here, what this life is all about, and why decisions made now will affect your eternity.

A PROMISE

The Plan involves a conflict, a spiritual conflict that started long ago in the Heavens and on the Earth. Most of humanity is oblivious to it; many do not have a clue.

Yet the conflict rages on, even now for a prize, that prize is "the individual souls of men."[7] For our benefit, God recorded the first key to understanding the Plan in the first *"Promise of Hope,"* sometimes referred to as the *"First Gospel"* given to man, this occurred in the Garden of Eden. After the fall, God first pronounced judgment on the serpent, and then the personage, who hid behind and used the serpent's body, that snake called "the Devil and Satan." God then pronounced judgment on the woman and then because of man, Adam's choice, He cursed the ground out of which they came and later returned. [8]

God gave the Promise to Eve after Satan, "The Deceiver," deceived her into eating "the forbidden fruit" of the tree of knowledge of good and evil, this she did, in direct disobedience to the command of God. She then gave it to her husband, and he ate, thus their acts of disobedience brought the entire human race under the dominion of Satan, sin, and death. However, we note with interest that Satan tempted and deceived Eve into sinning, and rebelling against the commandment. The foreknowledge of God said, *"And I will put enmity between you and the woman, and between your offspring and hers; He will crush your head, and you will strike His heel."* (See Genesis 3:15).

This verse is pregnant with meaning. For most believers understand this promise about Eve's offspring as speaking of the One Who would come into the world as "the Seed" of the woman to end the rebellion and do away with the curse of sin and death. Christ, the Son of God, the virgin born *"Seed* of the woman,"⁹ suffered a temporary wound on the Cross, but He dealt a fatal blow to the head of the serpent, that snake called "the Devil and Satan." Here God revealed the future conflict between the two offspring, the seed of good and evil, a conflict, which has only intensified since Christ defeated Satan at the Cross. Now the Apostle Peter speaking to a crowd of Jews gathered after the outpouring of the Holy Spirit at Pentecost spoke about the *"Seed."* He said, "This man was handed over to you by God's set purpose and foreknowledge; and you, with the help of wicked men, put Him to death by nailing Him to the Cross."¹⁰

(Note: the word "man" as used in this text sometimes refers to humanity; both man and woman).

The curses came on man because they violated the only commandment given them. By disobedience, Adam (man) lost his rule of dominion over the earth, as this was the enemies plan in the deception. Satan regained the dominion of the earth, which he previously lost in his fall, when the earth was (became) without form, and void; and darkness covered the face of the deep. (See Genesis 1:2). Through Adam's disobedience and fall, he (Satan) became "the god of this age," ¹¹ and "the ruler of this world." ¹² From the beginning it was a test, a test of obedience, and the man and woman failed. Today Satan and his "principalities, powers, and world-rulers, of darkness, and spiritual host of wickedness in heavenly places,"¹³ work through the many who mock,

> "GOD SENT HIS WORD; HE GAVE HIS ONLY BEGOTTEN SON. HE SENT CHRIST TO SET THE CAPTIVES FREE."

ridicule and attack those who believe the Biblical account given in God's Word. [14] God sent His Word; He gave His only begotten Son.[15] He sent Christ to *set the captives free* from the power of Satan and his kingdom of death and darkness, and free from the coming eternal damnation.[16] He came to set us free from the power and fear of death, and the temporal mind-set, by which Satan holds many captive.[17] He came to give us eternal life and a rich inheritance, a place in the Kingdom to come. For even now the powers of darkness are at work, through their many strongholds, for in these lasts days they influence and control men of a temporal mind-set. For even now manipulators, evil people, and false teachers continue to spring up motivated by self-interest, greed, and ignorance. As the Word says, "But evil people and impostors will flourish. They will go on deceiving others, and they themselves will be deceived."[18] While these deceivers are themselves deceived and led astray by Satan, God included a great deal of information on both, "the deceived and the Deceiver" in the Plan. Truth is, instead of an eternal, men have chosen a temporal worldview and therefore, a temporary life.

LIFE, TEMPORAL OR ETERNAL

God's Word exposes both the eternal and temporal minded.[19] The temporal minded see this world as the beginning and end, the eternal minded see life as the beginning with no end. The Owner- Creator gives us the real perspective on life in His Word; all others are temporary and false. For we came into this world, conditioned by a mind-set, which says, *"this is all there is."* Therefore, if this message, which permeates the world, is all that men know, how can they act and respond otherwise. There has to be more; for clarity, we must see beyond the veil.

> *How easy it is to want to give up and quit believing, when you cannot see the big picture and feel overwhelmed by the challenges of this life.'*

The Psalmist said, "My feet were slipping and I was almost gone. For I was envious of the prosperity of the proud and wicked. Yes, all through life, their road is smooth! They grow sleek and fat. They are not always in trouble and plagued with problems like everyone else, so their pride sparkles like a jeweled necklace, and their clothing is woven of cruelty! These fat cats have everything their hearts could wish for! They scoff at God and threaten His people. How proudly they speak!

They boast against the very heavens, and their words strut through the earth. And so, God's people are dismayed and confused, and drink it all in. "Does God realize what is going on?" they ask. "Look at these men of arrogance; they never have to lift a finger—theirs is a life of ease; and all the time their riches multiply."

Have I been wasting my time? Why take the trouble to be pure? All I get out of it is trouble every day and all day long! If I had really said that I would have been a traitor to your people. Yet it is so hard to explain— this prosperity of those that hate the LORD.

Then one day I went into God's sanctuary to meditate and thought about the future of these evil men. What a slippery path they are on—suddenly God will send them sliding over the cliff and down to their destruction, an instant end to all their happiness, an eternity of terror.

Their present life is only a dream! They will awaken to the truth as one awakens from a dream of things that never really were! When I saw this, what turmoil filled my heart!

I saw myself so stupid and ignorant; I must seem like an animal to you, O God. But even so, You love me! You are holding my right hand! You will keep on guiding me all my life with your wisdom and counsel; and afterward, receive me into the glories of Heaven! Who have I in heaven but You? And I desire no one on earth as much as You! My health fails; my spirits droop, Yet God remains!

He is the strength of my heart; He is mine forever! But those refusing to worship God will perish, for He destroys those serving other gods. But as for me, I get as close to Him as I can! I have chosen Him and will tell everyone about the wonderful ways He rescues me." [20]

Satisfied by the pleasures of this life many people never see the need to prepare themselves for the life to come. The temporal mind-set considers the idea of a personal God, One Who will one day return to judge this world in righteousness, [21] far too frightening or foolish for them to grasp, admit, or allow. It is so unbelievable to them; they reject the thought out of hand. People somehow hope that if they ignore the truth, it will go away, or by rejecting it, it will not affect them, but sadly, they could not be further from the truth. Without the Word of God, we would have had no idea what this life is all about, what God created us for, or why we are here.

"O the depth of weeping, wailing, and gnashing of teeth when many realize, "after it is too late," that this was the test of their life and they failed." [22]

GOD HAS GIVEN US THE PROMISE OF ETERNAL LIFE

God created the soul in man to live and last forever; our souls are eternal, but our bodies' just temporary houses. They are frail, vulnerable sheaths that wear out; they don't last for any noticeable amount of time, *"it's but a vapor, here one moment and gone the next."*[23] Even so, our time on earth is short, too, and our lives here spent on probation. "The days of our lives *are* seventy years; and if by reason of strength *they are* eighty years, yet their boast *is* only labor and sorrow; for it is soon cut off, and we fly away."[24]

There is a progression in the Plan. For those "born-again" born of the Spirit, there is the hope of a new everlasting body to replace this temporary one. The Scriptures says, "First the natural then the spiritual."[25] Because of this, "by faith" all believers from the beginning have placed their hope in God replacing this old temporary body, with a new resurrected everlasting one. [26]

Think of your body as the outer husk of a seed germ, the inner life, your spirit within being a seed. For the born again, that seed comes alive in Christ. Nevertheless, someone will say, *"How are the dead raised up? And with what body do they come?"* Foolish one, "What you sow is not made alive unless it dies. And what you sow, you do not sow that body that shall be, but mere grain–perhaps wheat or some other *grain*. But God gives it a body as He pleases, and to each seed its own body. All flesh *is* not the same flesh, but *there is* one *kind of* flesh of men, another flesh of animals, another of fish, *and* another of birds.

There are also celestial bodies, and terrestrial bodies; but the glory of the celestial *is* one, and the *glory* of the terrestrial *is* another. *There is* one glory of the sun, another glory of the moon, and another glory of the stars; for *one* star differs from *another* star in glory. *So also, is the resurrection of the dead.*

> *The body* is sown in corruption; it is raised in incorruption.
> It is sown in dishonor; it is raised in glory.
> It is sown in weakness; it is raised in power:
> It is sown a natural body; it is raised a spiritual body.
> There is a natural body, and there is a spiritual body.

And so, it is written, "The first man Adam became a living being." The last Adam became a life-giving spirit.

However, the spiritual is not first, but the natural, and afterward the spiritual. The first man *was* of the earth, *made* of dust; the second Man *is* the Lord from heaven. As *was* the *man* of dust, so also *are* those *who are made* of dust; and as *is* the heavenly *Man*, so also are those who are heavenly. And as we have borne the image of the man of dust, we shall bear the image of the heavenly *Man*." [27]

The Lord Himself said, "I assure you, anyone who believes in Me already has everlasting life."[28] I assure you, those who listen to My Message and believe in God Who sent Me have everlasting life. They will never be condemned for their sins, but they have already passed from death into life.[29]

Listen, God gave His Word to give us a new prospective, a new view on life, a "right" view of life. A change in perspective is the only cure; it is all about the Truth. The more truth we see in God's Plan, the more our prospective will change, until finally, *"we get it."*

His goal has always been that we see this life the way He sees it. Only in and through His Word, His Plan, can we begin to see Him for Whom He is, and us for whom we are. "God is Love."[30] Life is everlasting, only this phase is temporary. Love's motivation is Eternal. Satan, the "god of this age," [31] rules over men through ignorance of the truth, sin, death, and the fear of death. [32] His plan is to keep men bound up in a temporal worldview, therefore, a hopeless temporary existence. Once we see that God's Love is perfect, and there is no fear in Love, but perfect Love cast out all fear,[33] *"we get it."* Love covers a multitude of sins;[34] Love was victorious over death and the fear of death." Sin, death and the fear of death, frame the temporal mind-set.[35] Through ignorance of the truth, men remain in a temporal mind-set of sin and bondage; there is no freedom in sin or bondage. Jesus Christ is the One Who sets men free.[36] When we embrace the Son of God's Love, we embrace freedom and life. We know that He died so we might live, and that through His name we might have Eternal Life.[37]

BEFORE TIME BEGAN

The Plan of Salvation and Redemption unveils the foreknowledge of our Sovereign God. Everything that our Father wanted man to know is in "the Plan." God wrote the Plan through chosen men.[38] God gave the Bible with its many books to man in various times and various places, over the course of a 1600-year period of History. The "His" in History refers to Christ; it is all about "Him," and there is a consistency in purpose about Him, seen and revealed throughout the Plan. The many portraits in the various sixty-six books all point to Him and His work. Eternal life is what man lost in the garden, where obedience would have brought life, guaranteed blessing, and everlasting fellowship with our God and Father, disobedience brought death, a curse, and broken fellowship with the God of His Word.

God's foreordained purpose was to provide "Justification and Sanctification," setting apart those who through faith leading to obedience, would believe in the Plan, and walk in His grace and peace, just as faithful angels do now.[39] God knew from the beginning, before time began, everyone who would see and accept His glorious Plan of Salvation. "Not bound by time, the God of Eternity knows and declares the End from the Beginning."[40] Imagine the God of eternity, who transcends time, looking down through the ages and the corridors of time foreseeing everything as it would happen, "before it happened." He foresaw each person who would place his or her trust in the sacrifice of His only begotten Son. God, having offered His Son as the "sin sacrifice" for the Sins of the entire world, foresaw each one whom through faith and confession would believe in, and lay hold to the promise of pardon. God having printed their names into "the Lamb's Book of Life."[41] These are the Elect, the Chosen.[42]

"GOD KNEW FROM THE BEGINNING, BEFORE TIME BEGAN EVERYONE WHO WOULD SEE AND ACCEPT HIS GLORIOUS PLAN OF SALVATION."

Our Salvation rest on the foreknowledge of the Sovereign God Who holds the keys to His Plan. The Scripture says, "For those whom He foreknew *of whom He was aware and loved beforehand*, He also *destined from the beginning foreordaining them to be molded into the image of His Son* and share inwardly His likeness, that He might become the firstborn among many brethren."[43]

In other words, "For God knew His people in advance, and *He chose them to become like His Son,* so that His Son would be the firstborn, with many brothers and sisters.[44] This is the reason we cry out, "Abba Father."

The Sovereign God set in motion the foreordained Plan of Salvation to fulfill His immutable, unchanging purpose. It is He, "Who has saved us and called us to a holy life—not because of anything we have done but because of His Own Purpose and Grace. This Grace was given us in Christ Jesus BEFORE THE BEGINNING OF TIME."[45] The Plan has followed the secret, hidden wisdom of God. A wisdom not known in generation's past, or to the angels in the spirit realm. "No, we speak of God's secret wisdom, a wisdom that has been hidden and that God destined for our glory BEFORE TIME BEGAN."[46]

We base our Hope of Salvation on God's Message. He intended it to stimulate and promote the FAITH of His chosen ones. God's Plan is to lead us to a correct discernment, recognition of and acquaintance with the Truth, which belongs to, harmonizes with, and tends to godliness, resting in the Hope of Everlasting Life. Our purpose in this work is to look closely at those verses in the Plan which expound on the Promise of Hope, revealed in the Garden "of a Redeemer" who would come through the *"seed of the woman."* To reveal the God who Planned to give "the Promise," even before "the beginning of time."

In the letter to his disciple named Titus, the Apostle Paul wrote, "I have been sent to bring faith to those God has chosen and to teach them to know the truth that shows them how to live godly lives. This truth gives them the confidence of Eternal Life, which God promised them before the world began—and He cannot lie."[47]

He has set before us death and life, which will you choose.
Is yours a temporal, or an eternal view?

Have you accepted God's gift of Salvation?[48] Is your name in the Lambs Book of Life?[49] Have you confessed with your mouth the Lord Jesus and believed in your heart that God raised Him from the dead?[50] Have you asked Him to come and make your heart His home?

CHAPTER 2

An Outline of the Eternal Plan

"I am convinced: You can do anything and everything. Nothing and no one can upset Your Plans."[1] *"When I think of the wisdom and scope of God's Plan, I fall to my knees and pray to the Father,"*[2]

"THE MASTER PLAN DRAFTED"

At some point, long ago in the eternal past, before God called time, space, the spirit realm, and the material universe into existence, there was a high council meeting of the Godhead. In that meeting, God the Father, God the Son, and God the Holy Spirit as One, decided to begin the work of "The Master Plan." The Plan drafted, laid out the outline for Creation, and included everything from beginning to end. [3] The Plan involved creating a succession of realms, peopled by both visible and invisible created beings. All of whom, having eternal life, would live on in eternity, glorifying God in an everlasting, ever unfolding Kingdom. God, Himself, would begin a progression of ever unfolding unveilings.[4] Throughout eternity, God Planned to unveil many

> "THE PLAN INVOLVED CREATING A SUCCESSION OF REALMS, PEOPLED BY BOTH VISIBLE AND INVISIBLE CREATED BEINGS."

new and yet unspeakable creations, each with characteristics that we in our present state, cannot begin to fathom the depths of or begin to imagine. For starters, two groups of beings were the focus of God's purpose; these were the angels and man. In phase one of the Plan, God by direct creation, fashioned and formed a hierarchy and company of countless angelic beings, spirit beings made of spirit-material, invisible beings each varying in glory, character, and features.[5]

Phase two followed phase one of the Plan. In this phase God created the race of man, living souls covered by earthy-material, visible beings, they too would vary in appearance, abilities, character, and features, but unlike angels, they would increase in numbers through the act of *reproduction.*[6]

God planned every conceivable benefit for His Creation, in both spiritual and physical realms. The Plan involved creating everything in existence, both the visible and invisible realms, all non-living and living substances, down to the smallest particle and tiniest organism.

Now Creation has its roots in the character and qualities found in God. *God made laws and rules that placed limits on each creature, for the common good, order, and benefit of all.* These laws and rules perpetuate order and promote divine characteristics. Characteristics such as authority, obedience, love, joy, peace, kindness, goodness, faithfulness, gentleness, self-control,[7] faith, hope, trust, worship, praise, patience, virtue, holiness, righteousness, and perfection. These created beings would share in the rule over a living Eternal Kingdom.

God foresaw everything that would or could happen. God foresaw "disobedience" in the angels, one third of whom followed Lucifer, His highest angel in sin and rebellion,[8] He also foresaw the sin and fall of man.[9]

Therefore, God foreknew that He would not be able to set up His authority within the ranks of these free moral agents without an example. He had no interest in creating a race of robots, but creatures who exercised self-rule, and the power of choice; creatures who by choice want open and transparent fellowship with Him. For the good of His Creation, God Himself chose to unfold the principles of "Authority and Obedience."[10]

Now in both the Godhead and the Plan, the Father is the One in Authority, He is the head overall.[11] But authority without obedience is useless, since authority cannot exist alone. Therefore, God must show, by example, "the fruits of obedience and disobedience" to His created beings. Thus, having foreseen future events He decided the principle of authority would come by obedience in the Son. From this, we begin to learn the distinct roles of "God the Father," "God the Son," and "God the Holy Spirit."[12] After the rebellion in heaven (which we shall cover in detail, in other volumes of this work), "The Plan" has been to restore order to Creation, based on the principles of *"authority and obedience."*

After the fall of a group of angels, led by Satan in "the Rebellion," "the Master's Plan" called for bringing forth the second phase of the Plan— "creating the race of man." Human beings would reproduce, multiply, and refill the earth during the generations of their time.[13] This phase of the

Plan allowed every soul that came into the world through reproduction an opportunity, by choice and actions to be part of a future "restored" Creation.[14] Humanity would make their choice during a series of administration's (dispensations) of God's dealings and testing's, just as He had previously done with the angels (remember, there are good angels and bad angels).

It is during this phase that men with short life spans are undergoing a time of probation while still in physical (temporary) bodies, here on the earth. It is out from them that God has chosen those who have passed the test, having trusted in His Plan; the faithful, those declared righteous by faith in and through the work of God the Son.[15] Through them God is bringing His Master Plan to fruition.

Here is "a Body" of people born throughout the generations, chosen by God, from all over the earth who having heard responded yes to the Good News. The Bible calls them "the Church," "a called-out assembly" of the LORD. These are the souls of those chosen and redeemed out from every tribe, language, people, and nation.[16]

A body of people who by FAITH believed in God's Plan, while having experienced life in the flesh, they chose to live in Him, and He in them. [17] Their spiritual life rekindled by new birth, being *"Born-Again."* [18] They are now waiting for their eternal body.[19] In this life, they have come to Christ; they are the spiritual body in-dwelt by the LORD of Glory, those who will one day share in His Everlasting Love and Life. A body of believers who through spiritual adoption have become the children of God, [20] "a Holy Nation, a Royal Priesthood," [21] appointed to titles and positions in a restored Kingdom, "Our Fathers Kingdom, where Righteousness lives." [22]

This is the heritage and birthright of the people of FAITH, the tried, tested and approved. A chosen people fitted and prepared for roles as Royal Rulers and Priest in the Kingdom of our God.

CHAPTER 3

The Center of God's Incredible Plan

For I know the thoughts and plans that I have for you, says the LORD, thoughts and plans for welfare and peace and not for evil, to give you hope in your final outcome. Then you will call upon Me, and you will come and pray to Me, and I will hear and heed you. Then you will seek Me, inquire and require Me as a vital necessity and find Me when you search for Me with all of your heart.[1]

GOD LOVES YOU

Inspired by the Holy Spirit, in the first Chapter of Ephesians the Apostle Paul wrote, "That God devised the entire Plan of Salvation, "Before," He laid the foundation of the world, and this He did through Jesus Christ. He did it to fulfill the intense love with which He loved us."

The Plan which in eternity past existed in the mind of God, is the Plan unfolding in Creation through time. As we have said, God planned to produce Godly offspring (the born-again) who go from FAITH to RIGHTEOUSNESS. For the believer this is everlasting, never-ending life in His presence, joyfully loving, worshipping, and serving, "the God of our Salvation." Our hope is at the center of the Plan. But some may ask, "Why does God hide Himself?" The key to understanding is this, "Man's life on earth is one of probation." While on probation "Each one of us must decide," each person must choose to believe or not to believe; it's just that

> "THE KEY TO UNDERSTANDING IS THIS, "MAN'S LIFE ON EARTH IS ONE OF PROBATION." WHILE ON PROBATION "EACH ONE OF US MUST DECIDE,"

simple.[2] Every person must decide what he or she will do with Christ,[3] and yes, each one of us will have to give an account.[4] Now, for God to reveal

Himself (even though He has and does, in so many ways) would defeat the purpose of FAITH. He has revealed Himself in His Holy Word and in the person of His Son, Our Lord, and Savior Jesus Christ. God's Incredible Plan was not only for the Salvation of "the whosoever wills"[5] among humanity, the ones who would believe. He also gave it to Creation, to announce in advance, the Plan to end the rebellion and destroy the works of the Devil.[6]

All this also comes from the LORD Almighty, wonderful in counsel and magnificent in wisdom. [7] All of this is in, and uncovered in, His unfolding Plan.

The Plan is a revelation to angels and man of the qualities and the varied (multifaceted) wisdom,[8] and truth of our God, not only in making promises, but also in fulfilling His Word. God uses Satan, fallen angels, the world's social order and the tendency of man's fleshly nature to test man, revealing the folly of rebellion and the outcome of disobedience. It is by these same instruments, He tests the Faith of the sincere, through trials of fire, and in so doing, is bringing many sons and daughters to glory,[9] thus restoring order and fellowship with Himself and His Creation.

Through the many revelations in the Word, we see the outline and details of "The Master's Plan," His Will and Purposes for Creation and His honoring His Word, holding it above His Name.[10]

The Father knows that this phase, "this Present Age," of the Plan for Creation will fail, ending in judgment, and destruction; He has already told us so. Not because He doesn't care, far from it, but because sin, rebellion (the spirit of sin), disobedience, and death are still in the world, this is why He created judgment.[11] Nevertheless, you and I can rest assured that God has a better plan for us, a "Master Plan."

A LOOK AT HIS-STORY

God's Plan for His Creation, as outlined in the Bible, stands alone. Whether the Old or New Testament, it is all about Him. "He is Lord."[12] Scriptures reveal, "The Christ, the Son of God" throughout. "His-Story, given and preserved over the years for us. God recorded It for our benefit and example, thus allowing us to develop a personal faith in Him." [13] Those who have come to know Him have placed their hope "in Him." He is the anchor of our soul, both sure and steadfast,[14] thus, through fellowship with Him, we can learn and mirror that attitude and manner of living, which is just like His, one of humility, trust, and obedience. We give thanks to the Father through Him.

LET'S TAKE A BRIEF LOOK AT WHAT CHRIST DID:

At the appointed time, God the Son emptied Himself; He laid down His power and left Heaven's glory to be made flesh. [15] The birth of the Lord Jesus Christ was "God coming forth." God became a man. God the Son, "Who, being in very nature God, did not consider equality with God as something to be grasped, but made Himself nothing, taking the very nature of a servant, being made in human likeness. And being found in appearance as a man He humbled Himself and became obedient to death—even death on a cross! Therefore, God exalted Him to the highest place and gave Him the Name that is above every name, that at the name of Jesus every knee should bow, in heaven and on earth and under the earth, and every tongue confess that Jesus Christ is Lord, to the Glory of God the Father." [16]

Now, the Scriptures urge us to "Let this mind be in you, which was also in Christ Jesus." [17] *He made Himself of no reputation.* Because the Son was God, He did not look on His sharing of God's nature as robbery. That is, He did not see His nature as God, "as something to be seized or grasped," as though He did not have it, or as "a thing to be held," as though He might lose it. We know that instead of staying as God with power and authority, motivated by love, He came to man's side, to be God's example, and to light the way, so men might follow.[18]

HE TOOK ON THE LIKENESS OF MEN

He accepted all the limits of man, taking the form of a slave. "God became a man." In the incarnation Christ being God, added to His nature that of a bondservant, the lowest status on the social ladder, and the exact opposite of His position as the Lord of Glory. We know that for the sake of the kingdom and Creation, God had to show the principles of authority and obedience by example to His creatures. We also know that man through disobedience and sin closed the door of open fellowship with his Creator. Therefore, the Lord came into the world that He Created. Through birth, He made Himself in the likeness of man. He who was fully God became fully man. Born with all the characteristics of man, He came to earth to identify with man. "The Word became flesh,"[19] He came to become God's symbol of obedience. Since disobedience, sin, and rebellion originated in created beings, to save the race, obedience must be shown in a created being.

HE HUMBLED HIMSELF

Jesus willingly took on the role of a servant, if someone said that God forced Him, *"Then let Love be guilty."* He loved us so we, by His example, would see and learn to love one another, even as He loved us.[20] In His humility, He revealed God's *"agape"*—unconditional love[21] for the fallen race of man, His humility, and sacrifice served as an example for all Creation.

HE WAS OBEDIENT TO THE POINT OF DEATH

For "greater love has no one than this, than to lay down one's life for his friends." [22]

Although born a man, He was sinless. He never sinned and did not deserve to die. Because of sin, God appointed all men to die, and afterwards, "the Judgment."[23] But there was hope, for in the Purpose of God we find the "Law of Reciprocity." "For you know the grace of our Lord Jesus Christ, that, though He was rich, yet for your sakes He became poor, that you through His poverty might become rich."[24] Christ chose to become poor, so we might become rich. He chose to die, so we might live. He willingly chose to lay down His life, so He could charge the sins of the world to His account.[25] Because He was sinless, He could credit His righteousness to the accounts of all who believe in Him.[26]

Now the Lord could have returned to Glory in one of two ways. One way was to obey unreservedly as man, on all occasions, through all the trials and temptations, without the slightest hint of rebellion. Walking step-by-step in obedience to the authority of God the Father, "In doing so He would become Lord of all." Should He become disobedient, however, in even the slightest degree on earth as a man, He would still be able to reclaim His place in the Godhead by asserting His original authority. However, this would have forever destroyed the principle of obedience, closing the door to our Salvation. Now the Lord discarded the second path and walked humbly in the way of obedience, even obedience to the point of death.

HE DIED ON A CROSS

Having emptied Himself of His Power and Glory, He refused to fill Himself again. He never took an uncertain course. Instead, He bore in His body the sins of the entire world.

In the garden of Gethsemane, He sweats great drops of blood. [27] With anguish, He looked forward to the Cross. [28] Betrayed by one of His disciples,

[29] captured and carried away like a common criminal, [30] falsely accused, [31] taken and beaten beyond recognition, mocked and spat on, [32] crowned with a crown of thorns forced on His head. [33] They whipped and beat Him mercilessly. (See Isaiah 53).

Can you see the Creator willingly subjecting Himself to the hands of His Creation, and their destroying His body?

In the end, they subjected Christ to the cruelest form of execution, punishment reserved for the worst of criminals (The victim usually died after two or three days of agonizing suffering, enduring thirst, exhaustion, exposure, and eventual suffocation). He died, His body nailed to a cross.[34] *Prophetically*, in the cross, we see the serpent striking His heel, and in the resurrection, His heel delivering a fatal blow to the serpent's head.[35]

THE FATHER HAS HIGHLY EXALTED HIM

It is because of what Christ did; "He, Who humbled Himself, God has highly exalted."[36] Having surrendered His divine power and glory and taking the form of a slave. Had the Lord failed in the way of obedience, He would never have returned with Glory. We would still be lost in our sins and trespasses; [37] He would have failed in setting the captives free. [38] Thus, only by obedience as a man, did He go back to heaven, having trained His disciples, He gave them the "Great Commission" to spread, "The Good News." [39] Thus, it was by victory that He returned,[40] by perfect and singular obedience, fulfilling God's purpose in the Master Plan. As a result, God has exalted Him and made Him Lord. When He returned to Glory, He did not fill Himself with the reputation that He once had, but it was God the Father Who brought this man into Glory. Now God the Son, in His return to Glory, is "Jesus the man."[41] We note that it was Jesus, "God the Son," who humbled Himself to become God's obedient servant, and "God the Father," who exalted Him to the place of highest Honor and Authority.[42] Also, for us, He satisfied God's just demands for the penalty of sin.[43]

GOD GAVE HIM "A NAME ABOVE ALL NAMES"

Therefore, "the name of Jesus is most precious;" there is no one else in Creation like Him. He is, "the God-man." When on the cross, He shouted, "IT IS FINISHED!"[44] He proclaimed to Creation not only the carrying out of God's Plan of Salvation, but He fulfilled all that His name means. For even before His birth, the prophecy went forth which said, "And you shall call His name JESUS, for He will save His people from their sins."[45] His death on the cross marked the triumph and victory of the Master's Plan and God's Love. (See Ephesians 1:15-23).

UNIVERSALLY RECOGNIZED AS LORD OF ALL

"Therefore, God exalted Him to the highest place of honor and gave Him the Name that is above every name, that at the name of Jesus every knee should bow, in heaven and on earth and under the earth and every tongue confess that Jesus Christ is Lord, to the Glory of God the Father." He is LORD as well as God. His being Lord speaks of His place with God the Father; the Father exalted Him. He is "the Master," having received all Power and Authority in heaven and on earth. His being God reveals His place in the Church, Israel, and the Creation. (See 1 Corinthians 15:20-28).

HOW WILL YOU ENTER ETERNITY?

How will you leave this world? In what state, is it either "saved or unsaved?" In the end, those who trust and obey have placed their hope in His Plan, while those who have rejected and ignored it will neither receive it, nor understand.

At the end of our time here on earth, all souls leave this world and enter the dominion of death and the grave, a waiting period of separation of the soul from the body. In the end, God will bring all souls, clothed into one of two judgments, either "the Judgment Seat of Christ" or "the Great White Throne Judgment." Choices and decisions made during our time of probation here on the earth, decide which of the two judgments in which we must appear. For what many do not see is the choice was not just for Adam and Eve, their story serves as a historical account and example. We, too, must make a choice (this is why minister's press for converts), we live or die by choice. God made away for all through, "Jesus Christ, He is our, Tree of Life."

Each of us must decide if we are going to "take and eat."

It is through Him alone that we enter a new life. This present Age and present life are not our real and complete life; it is only a step along the journey. Only by Faith in God, in the person of His Son, Jesus Christ, can you make the right choice.

Jesus said, "For God so loved the world that He gave His only begotten Son, that whoever believes in Him should not perish but have everlasting life."[46]

God loves you and has a glorious plan for your life; "Eternal Life, is your true-life." You must believe and confess this daily! Satan has a plan for your life also; his plan is to ruin God's Plan for you. He hates each person who loves the Word of Truth and labors intensely against them, to make them feel worthless and hopeless. He does not want anyone to believe or receive the truth that God dearly loves us, and no matter what happens, you and I are not alone, for He promised to never leave nor forsake us. He has been there for us more than we will ever know on this side of life.

As we will see, the Sovereign One, the Lord of all Creation, the One we worship, did it all; He put the entire world in place, He set the stage, and everything around us. He did it for us to test us, to prove us, and to give us life. His Plans and Purposes for our lives go far beyond Salvation, or anything this present world can hope to offer.

"Long ago, even before He made the World, God chose us to be His very own, through what Christ would do for us; He decided then to make us holy in His eyes, without a single fault—who stand before Him covered in His Love."[47]

You did not choose Me, but I chose you and appointed you that you should go and bear fruit, and that your fruit should remain, that whatever you ask the Father in My name He may give you. These things I command you, that you love one another.[48]

Part 2 –

"The Sovereign One"

CHAPTER 4

The Sovereign One

The LORD REIGNS, He is robed in Majesty; the LORD is robed in Majesty and is armed with Strength. The World is firmly established; it cannot be moved. Your throne was established long ago; You are from all Eternity. [1]

SOVEREIGNTY, THE ETERNAL REIGN OF THE LORD

The greatest and most important idea that a person can entertain, is the possibility of a real and personal Sovereign God. The God who sent His Son to die for the sins of the world. [2] Not only will our response to this truth govern the way we live down here, but it will also forever fix our eternal destiny. Unless one satisfactorily answers the "Who" question of his or her own existence, he or she cannot answer the What, When, Where, How and Why. The Prophet Isaiah wrote, "In the year that King Uzziah died, I saw the Lord seated on a throne, high and exalted, and the train of His robe filled the temple. Above Him were seraphs, each with six wings: With two wings they covered their faces, with two they covered their feet, and with two they were flying. And one cried to another and said: 'Holy, Holy, Holy is the LORD of Hosts; the whole earth is full of His Glory!" [3] Isaiah went on to write, "And the posts of the door were shaken by the voice of him who cried out, and the house was filled with smoke. So I said: 'Woe is me, for I am undone! Because I am a man of unclean lips, and I dwell in the midst of a people of unclean lips; For my eyes have seen the King, the LORD of Hosts."' [4] Because He saw the LORD, Isaiah realized in the instant of that moment, both who he was, and who God IS. He saw the transcendent awe-inspiring One; the One who is indescribable, beyond words. Each one of us will one day behold what Isaiah saw.

THE SOVEREIGN GOD OF ETERNITY

The earth is the LORD's, and everything in it. The world and all its people belong to Him.[5] The Lord says, "For all the animals of field and forest are Mine! The cattle on a thousand hills! And all the birds upon the mountains… for all the world is Mine, and everything in it!" [6] The heavens are Yours, the world, everything—for You created them all.[7] The LORD God is Sovereign, He reigns, and rules over everything, everything that has ever existed and everything that ever will. As CREATOR of all, He is Supreme RULER overall.

He is God Who makes Plans and carries out those Plans.

His Plans and Purposes are everlasting in scope, what He does; He does for the greatest good and order of all His Creation. He is a God of knowledge, everything there is to know, past, present, and future, He knows. He is the God who knew the end from the beginning. [8] In His hand is the life of every Creature and the breath of all Mankind.[9] Jesus said, "Are not two sparrows sold for a penny? Yet not one of them can fall to the ground apart from our Father's will, notice, and consent. Again, we speak of His complete knowledge when we realize that. "Not only does He know the number of hairs on each of our heads, but He

> "NOT ONLY DOES HE KNOW THE NUMBER OF HAIRS ON EACH OF OUR HEADS, BUT HE ALSO KNOWS THE NUMBER OF EACH HAIR SHAFT."

also knows the number of each hair shaft." (See Matthew 10:29, 30). All this knowledge and detail went into making the Eternal Plan. Taken a step further, He is the Master Programmer of all DNA (we will cover this in more detail, in the chapter on "Intelligent Designs"). While "many want to be gods" there is only one real "God." He declares Himself the only true God, and there is no other, the Scriptures proclaim, "But the LORD is the only true God, the living God. He is the everlasting King! The whole earth trembles at His anger. The nations hide before His wrath. Say this to those who worship other gods: 'Your so-called gods, who did not make the heavens and earth, will vanish from the earth.' But God made the earth by His Power, and He preserves it by His Wisdom. He has stretched out the heavens by His Understanding."[10] Of the Sovereign God, Job said, "Nevertheless, His mind concerning me is still unchanged, and who can turn Him from His purposes? Whatever He wants to do, He does. So, He will do for me all He has Planned. He controls my destiny."[11]

The LORD is Sovereign, not bound by time; He is the Master over time. He is Eternal; He is the First and the Last,[12] "Who has prepared and done this, calling forth and guiding the destinies of the generations *of the nations* from the beginning? I, the LORD—the First *existing before history began* and with the Last *an ever-present, unchanging God*—I Am He."[13]

The Nature of God

Now about God's nature, the Holy Spirit inspired men to write and reveal the following truth:

"Our God is One."

In the Old Testament, Moses inspired and anointed by the Holy Spirit wrote, "Hear, O Israel: The LORD our God, the LORD is One! You shall love the LORD your God with all your heart, and with all your soul, and with all your strength."[14]

God gave us His Word so, "that all the people of the earth may know that the LORD is God, and that there is none else."[15] The Scriptures challenge the false or would be gods and those who promote them, those who say, *"There are many gods, therefore many paths to glory, and the life after this one."* Those promoting such views are false teachers.

THE NAMES AND TITLES OF GOD

"There is only One True and Living God, and there is none like Him. He is Eternal, infinite in being and perfection. He is the Sovereign One, the Ruler over all Creation working all things according to the counsel of His Immutable and Most Righteous Purpose, Plan, and Will. This He does for His glory and our good.

He is the God of Heaven and Earth. The I AM that I AM; the God of Abraham, Isaac, and Jacob; The Ancient of Days; The LORD God of Host. He is the Majestic One. He is the KING OF KINGS AND LORD OF LORDS. The Alpha and Omega, the First and Last, the Beginning and End. He is the Word of God, the Author of our Salvation and the Author and Finisher of our Faith, the Author of all True Prophecy.

He is the Almighty, Omnipotent- "all-powerful," Omniscient- "all knowing," Omnipresent- "everywhere present." He is the Compassionate Creator, the Provider and Sustainer, the Preserver, Revealer and Redeemer. The Father of us all. He is the Rewarder of them that diligently seek Him. He is the Hearer and Answerer of Prayer. The God of all Comfort and

Grace. He is Unfathomable, Unsearchable, Unchangeable, and Dependable. The Faithful One, the Source of Love, Knowledge, Wisdom, and Truth. He is the Way, the Truth, and the Life.

He is the Light, The Savior of mankind, the Rock, our Refuge and Hiding Place. He is Our Deliverer and Strength, our Buckler and Shield. The Horn of our Salvation. He is our High Tower. He is our Mediator and Intercessor, our Sanctifier, our Healer, Rich in Goodness and Truth. The Only Righteous God, He is our Righteousness, the Amen.

He is Worthy of Worship and Praise, Blessing, and Glory Wisdom, Thanksgiving, Honor, Power, Riches, and Might. He is Wonderful, Counselor, Mighty God, Everlasting Father, and the Prince of Peace. He is Invisible, Invincible, Immutable, Immense, and Incomprehensible. The Most Loving, and Most Gracious, the Most High, the Most Glorious, the Most Wise, Most Free, Most Absolute, Most Pure Spirit. The Most Holy, the Holy One.

He is Merciful, Long-suffering, ready to Pardon, the Forgiver of Iniquity, Transgression, and Sin. He is the Just Judge, the LORD of Justice, Most Terrible, and Just in His Judgments. Hating All Sin, and Who will by no means clear the Guilty."

God is Spirit

He is incorporeal, invisible, without fleshly or material substance, without physical parts or passions; He is free from the temporal limits of space and time. Those who worship Him can do so any time, any place, worship is a matter of the heart. Jesus said, "The true worshippers will worship the Father in spirit and in truth; for the Father is seeking such to worship Him. God is Spirit, and those who worship Him must worship in spirit and in truth."[16]

God is a Person

Throughout His Word God displays all the qualities of personality just as they appear in man, namely mind (intellect), will, and emotion. Now this is only fitting in the sense that God created the first man, in His Own image.

For example, *God Creates,* "He created Heaven and the Earth." *And He Destroys,* "He destroyed Sodom and Gomorrah."

God Provides, "These all wait for You, to give them their food at the proper time. When You give it to them, they gather it up; when You open Your hand, they are satisfied with good things." *And He Withholds,* "When

You hide Your face, they are terrified; when You take away their breath, they die and return to the dust. When You send Your Spirit, they are created, and You renew the face of the earth." [17]

God Loves, "For God so loved the world that He gave His One and only Son, {Or His only begotten Son} that whoever believes in Him shall not perish but have Eternal Life."[18] *And He Hates,* "There are six things the LORD hates, seven that are detestable to Him"[19]

God Promotes, "No one from the east or the west or from the desert can exalt a man." [20] "Humble yourselves, therefore, under God's mighty hand, that He may lift you up in due time." [21] *And He Debases,* "But it is God Who judges: He brings one down, He exalts another." [22]

God Rejoices, "The LORD your God is with you, He is mighty to save. He will take great delight in you, He will quiet you with His love, He will Rejoice over you with singing." [23] "I will rejoice in doing them good and will assuredly plant them in this land with all My heart and soul." [24] *And He Grieves,* "The LORD was grieved that He had made man on the earth, and His heart was filled with pain." [25]

God Hears Sees, and Knows, "Does He Who implanted the ear not Hear? Does He who formed the eye not See? Does He Who disciplines Nations not punish? Does He who instructs man lack knowledge?" [26] *God Cares* "Cast all your anxiety on Him because He cares for you." [27] All the qualities that would show us what God is like, He revealed in His Word, the man Jesus Christ.

GOD IS IN CONTROL

God is still in control, everything in Creation held together by His Word. God's Word is the power by which the living God works out His Plans and Purposes in Creation, if God said it, He is going to do it; there is nothing that can stop Him. God said, "I have made the earth, and created man on it: I—My hands, stretched out the heavens, and all their Host I have commanded." [28] Because men do not see the hand of the invisible God, they think that either He doesn't exist, or He doesn't care. Ecclesiastes 8:11 says, *"Because the sentence against an evil work is not executed speedily, therefore the heart of the sons of men is fully set in them to do evil."* This verse reveals a God Who carries out judgment. Proverbs 1:7 says, "The fear of the LORD is the beginning of knowledge, but fools despise wisdom and instruction." Proverbs 9:10 (AMP), says, "The reverent and worshipful fear of the Lord is the beginning (the chief and choice part) of Wisdom, and the knowledge of the Holy One is insight and understanding." Sadly, what men do not realize is that He both exists and cares and is taking all our acts into account. He watches and waits; He is still in control.

"'O, if men only knew that God was watching and taking all our deeds into account, how many outcomes would be different."

A SOVEREIGN GOD DOES WHAT HE CHOOSES, ACCORDING TO HIS WILL

God is not a respecter of persons; "All the people of the earth are nothing compared to Him. He has the power to do as He pleases among the angels of heaven and with those who live on earth. No one can stop Him or challenge Him, saying, 'What do You mean by doing these things?'" [29] "If He sends death to snatch someone away, who can stop Him? Who dares to ask Him, 'What are You doing?'" [30] "The LORD does whatever pleases Him throughout all heaven and earth, and on the seas and in their depths." [31]

Sovereignty over Creation

God is Sovereign, "For He says to Moses," "I will show mercy to anyone I choose, and I will show compassion to anyone I choose." [32] (See Exodus 33:19). Having quoted Moses in this passage in Romans, Paul went on to say, "Well then, you might say, 'Why does God blame people for not listening? Haven't they simply done what He made them do?'" [33] However, the Apostle responded saying, "No, do not say that. Who are you, a mere human being, to criticize God? Should the thing that was created say to the one who made it, 'Why have you made me like this?' When a potter makes jars out of clay, doesn't he have a right to use the same lump of clay to make one jar for decoration and another to throw garbage into? God has every right to exercise His judgment and His power, but He also has the right to be very patient with those who are the objects of His judgment and are fit only for destruction. He also has the right to pour out the riches of His glory upon those He prepared to be the objects of His mercy—even upon us, whom He selected, both from the Jews and from the Gentiles. [34]

God says, "I Am the One Who exposes the false prophets as liars by causing events to happen that are contrary to their predictions. I cause wise people to give bad advice, thus proving them to be fools." [35] "These are people wise in their own eyes, but not wise toward the Lord." "He brings PRINCES to naught and reduces the RULERS of THIS WORLD to nothing." [36] "The king's heart is like a stream of water directed by the

LORD; He turns it wherever He pleases. [37] "He decides the course of world events; He removes kings and sets others on the throne. He gives wisdom to the wise and knowledge to the scholars." [38] "It is God alone who judges; He decides who will rise and who will fall." [39] In His hands is the life of every living thing and the breath of all mankind.[40]

While men and angels make choices, so does God, and God will bring about the predetermined outcome of His Plan. "In His hand are the life of every living thing and the breath of all mankind. Is it not the task of the ear to discriminate between *wise and unwise* words, just as the mouth distinguishes *between desirable and undesirable* food? With the aged *you say* is wisdom, and with the length of days comes understanding. But *only* with *God* are *perfect* wisdom and might; He *alone* has *true* counsel and understanding. Behold, He tears down, and it cannot be built again; He shuts a man in, and none can open. He withholds the waters, and the land dries up; again, He sends forth *rains*, and they overwhelm the land or transform it. With Him are might and wisdom; the deceived and the deceiver are His *and in His power.* He leads *great and scheming* counselors away stripped and barefoot and makes the judges fools *in human estimation, by overthrowing their plans.* He looses the fetters *ordered* by kings and has *the* waistcloth *of a slave* bound about their *own* loins. He leads away priests as spoil, and men firmly seated He overturns. He deprives of speech those who are trusted and takes away the

> "HE LEADS GREAT AND SCHEMING COUNSELORS AWAY STRIPPED AND BAREFOOT AND MAKES THE JUDGES FOOLS IN HUMAN ESTIMATION, BY OVERTHROWING THEIR PLANS."

discernment and discretion of the aged. He pours contempt on princes and loosens the belt of the strong *disabling them, bringing low the pride of the learned.* He uncovers deep things out of darkness and brings into light black gloom and the shadow of death. He makes nations great, and He destroys them; He enlarges nations *and then straightens and shrinks them again* and leads them *away captive.* He takes away understanding from the leaders of the people of the land and of the earth and causes them to wander in a wilderness where there is no path. They grope in the dark without light, and He makes them to stagger and wander like a drunken man." [41]

He Commands and Controls Nature (the environment)

The earth is teaming with life. Stop and consider just how life happens to work, even with the vast variety of people on the earth. People live today, just as they have for thousands of years, under an assortment of settings and conditions, man's nature is the same now as it was then. Stop and think for a moment, can you see His hand of providence, in the care of all nature and Creation. "He causes the grass to grow for the cattle, and vegetation for the service of man, that He may bring forth food from the earth; And wine that makes glad the heart of man, oil to make his face shine, and bread which strengthens man's heart. The trees of the LORD are full of sap; the cedars of Lebanon, which He planted, where the birds make their nests; the stork has her home in the fir trees. The high hills are for the wild goats; the cliffs are a refuge for the rock badgers. He appointed the moon for seasons; the sun knows it's going down. You make darkness, and it is night, in which all the beasts of the forest creep about. The young lions roar after their prey and seek their food from God.

When the sun rises, they gather, and lie down in their dens. Man goes out to his work and to his labor until the evening. O LORD, how manifold are Your works! In wisdom You made them all. The earth is full of Your possessions. This great and wide sea, in which there are innumerable teeming things, living things that are both small and great. There the ships sail about; there is that Leviathan which You have made to play there. These all wait for You, that You may give them their food in due season.[42]

He Commands and Controls the Weather

Again, stop for a moment and think of all the various weather and climatic conditions going on around the earth right now. We see rain, thunderstorms, snow, windstorms, desert heat, sunshine, bitter cold all going on at any given time around the earth. After Noah's flood, God made a Covenant with Noah and his family saying, "As long as the earth remains, there will be springtime and harvest, cold and heat, winter and summer, day and night."[43] Since the days of Noah, "He never left himself without a witness. There were always His reminders, such as sending you rain and good crops and giving you food and joyful hearts."[44] He gave us the four seasons; He clothes the trees and plants in the spring and summer, removing their covering during fall and winter. That He has been faithful to what He promised, should be obvious to all who see. This is more proof of His faithfulness.

It is precisely because He is Sovereign that, "Whatever the LORD pleases He does, in heaven, and in earth, in the seas, and all deep places. He causes the vapors to ascend from the ends of the earth; He makes lightning for the rain; He brings the wind out of His treasuries." [45] It is God, "Who covers the heavens with clouds, Who prepares rain for the earth, Who makes grass to grow on the mountains." [46] He sends the snow like white wool; He scatters frost upon the ground like ashes. He hurls the hail like stones. Who can stand against His freezing cold? Then, at His command, it all melts. He sends His winds, and the ice thaws.[47]

THE SOVEREIGN ONE IS WORTHY OF HIGHEST PRAISE

Let all those who seek You rejoice and be glad in You; Let such as love Your salvation say continually, "The LORD be Magnified!" [48]

Prayer and Praise

God created us for Worship; He created us so we might offer up the sacrifice of *Praise*. When you see where the Plan is going, it will then dawn on you who we are. We are "a Chosen People, a Royal Priesthood, a Holy Nation, a people belonging to God that you may declare the *Praises* of Him Who called you out of darkness into His wonderful light." [49] "In Him," we have something exciting, exciting beyond ordinary, something wonderful, beyond extraordinary, and welling up within us in unspeakable *Joy*. When you see the Plan, His Master Plan for Creation, when it all comes together and clicks, in one of those, "Ah-ha" moments, one of those burning in the heart, raise your voice in *Praise* and shout for *Joy* moments." Then you will shout giving *Praise* and *Thanksgiving* to Him for all that He has done. — *"Then you've got it."* In that moment of amazement, you will know why we *Praise* Him. Your desire will be to walk with Him daily, 'Loving Him with all your heart, with all your soul, with your entire mind.' (See Matthew 22:37). When you realize just how much He loves us, you will know what it means to worship Him in spirit and in truth.

We *Praise* Him for Whom He is, for He is worthy of the highest *Praise*. We give *Praise* and thanksgiving to Him Who made the heavens, the earth and the seas and everything in them. This is what the Church did after Pentecost, when the Apostles using His name, saw the healing of a lame man. They gave testimony to the power of the name of Jesus. When the people heard this, they raised their voices together in a *Prayer of Praise*. (See Acts 4:24).

"*Praise the LORD*," for our LORD inhabits the *Praises* of His people. "Draw close to God, and He will draw close to you," we draw close to feel His presence, and bask in His strength. As His children, we draw close to renew our spiritual strength; we draw close for daily doses of encouragement as we walk through the battlegrounds of this present evil age.

Far too many saints are powerless to do good works, because they do not wrestle in *Prayer*. They do not ask or know what the Will of the LORD is, or what He would have them do to bring glory and honor to His name on earth. Many do not follow up on answered *Prayers*, with *Praise*, giving thanksgiving and glory to God for the outcome of what we *Prayed*. We need power from on high to do His Will, as we go forth as ministers of His Word. That power comes to us from and through *Praising the LORD*. (Read Psalms 145-150, these are *Psalms of Praise*).

Try *Praising* Him, Lift your hands, Lift your voice in *thanksgiving* to God for all He has done, bring your petitions, and return to the LORD. Say to him, "Forgive all our sins and graciously receive us, so that we may offer you *the sacrifice of Praise*." 50 "Practice your *Praise* to the LORD", "Continually offer from your lips *the sacrifice of Praise*, "do it now" and see what happens, test the LORD and see if He won't in turn give you strength and *Joy* with it. The voice of the Church is the voice of Worship and *Praise;* it is the voice of the Bride. It is the voice of joy and the voices of gladness, the voice of the bridegroom, and the voice of the bride, the voice of those who will say, PRAISE the Lord!

Praise the Lord from the heavens, *Praise* Him in the heights! *Praise* Him, all His angels, *Praise* Him, all His hosts! *Praise* Him, sun, and moon, *Praise* Him, all you stars of light! *Praise* Him, you highest heavens and you waters above the heavens! Let them *Praise* the name of the Lord, for He commanded, and they were Created. He also set them up forever and ever; He made a decree which shall not pass away *He fixed their bounds which cannot be passed over.*

Praise the Lord from the earth, you sea monsters and all deeps! You lightning, hail, fog, and frost, you stormy wind fulfilling His orders! Mountains and all hills, fruitful trees, and all cedars! Beasts and all cattle, creeping things and flying birds! Kings of the earth and all peoples, princes and all rulers and judges of the earth! Both young men and maidens, old men, and children!

Let them *Praise* and exalt the name of the Lord, for His name alone is exalted and supreme! His glory and majesty are above earth and heaven! He has lifted a horn for His people *giving them power, prosperity, dignity, and preeminence,* a song of *Praise* for all His godly ones, for the people of Israel, who are near to Him. *Praise the Lord!* (Hallelujah!) [51]

Prayer and Praise should be the frame outlining our present life. For from Him, and through Him and to Him are all things. For all things originate with Him and come from Him; all things live through Him, and all things center in and tend to consummate and to end in Him. To Him be glory forever! Amen (so be it).[52] Through Him, therefore, let us constantly and always offer up to God *a sacrifice of Praise,* which is the fruit of lips that *thankfully* acknowledge and confess and glorify His name.[53]

"You are worthy, O Lord our God, to receive glory and honor and power. For you created everything, and it is for your pleasure that they exist and were created."[54]

"I will always bless the LORD: His praise shall continually be in my mouth. My soul shall make her boast in the LORD: the humble shall hear thereof and be glad. O magnify the LORD with me and let us exalt His name together." (Psalms 34:1-3).

CHAPTER 5

The Trinity – A closer look at God

For there are three that bear record in Heaven, the Father, the Word, and the Holy Ghost: and these three are One. And there are three that bear witness in earth, the Spirit, and the water, and the blood: and these three agree in One.1

෨෫෨ THE FATHER, SON, AND HOLY SPIRIT ෫෨෫෨

The unfolding nature of "The Plan" has done much to reveal the otherwise hidden nature of God. For while, there is only One God, there are three eternal people, "Father, Son, and Holy Spirit," who although distinct in position and role stand as One in substance and purpose. They together make the Godhead. While you cannot find the word "Trinity" in the Bible, the following Scriptures reveal there is more than One person in the Godhead: God Himself revealed this when He said, "Let *Us* make man in *Our* Image, In *Our* likeness," [2] And the LORD God said, "The man has now become Like One of *Us*, knowing good and evil." [3] Again the Lord said, "Come, Let *Us* go down and there confuse their language, that they may not understand one another's speech." [4] And, Then I heard the voice of the LORD saying, "Whom shall I send? And Who will Go for *Us*?" [5]

The Triune God has revealed Himself in three Persons, the Father, the Son, and the Holy Spirit.

All three persons of the Godhead are carrying the Eternal Plan forward, each performing specific roles, each sharing in the task of Creation, Redemption and Restoring order to God's Eternal Kingdom. Overtime men have proposed various illustrations trying to explain the Trinity. To provide our own illustration and comparison, let us look at the quality of "Love," contrasted with the types of rays, coming from the Sun. The Sun is one, and yet it produces heat, light, and chemical rays (chemical reactions producing the effect called photosynthesis).

God is Love. By way of comparison, let us use the Sun to reveal the members of the Trinity and show how They manifest the Love of God. The Sun produces heat; while we can feel the heat of the sun, we cannot see it, 'the Father' is like the heat of the Sun, we can feel the warmth of His Love. The Sun produces light, we can see light, but we can't feel it, 'the Son' is like the light of the Sun, having come in the flesh, He came to reveal Gods Love, He said of Himself, "I Am the Light of the world." He is the visible representative of the Godhead, in Christ, we see God's Love. When Philip, one of the disciples, said, "Lord, show us the Father, and we will be satisfied." Jesus said to him, "Have I been with you so long, and yet you have not known Me, Philip? He who has seen Me has seen the Father; so how can you say, 'Show us the Father'?" [6] *Jesus came to reveal the Father.* Light from the Sun allows us to see. The Sun also produces

> "HAVE I BEEN WITH YOU SO LONG, AND YET YOU HAVE NOT KNOWN ME, PHILIP? HE WHO HAS SEEN ME HAS SEEN THE FATHER;"

chemical rays, which we can neither see nor feel. "The Holy Spirit" produces the chemical reaction. He gives life and power. In nature, photosynthesis is how green plants, and certain organisms use the energy of light to convert carbon dioxide and water into simple sugar glucose. In so doing, photosynthesis provides the basic energy source for all life forms. An important product of photosynthesis is oxygen, on which all life depends. Thus, all life on earth, directly or indirectly, depends on photosynthesis as a source of food, energy, and oxygen, making it one of the most important biochemical processes known. The Holy Spirit is the source of spiritual life (food, energy, and oxygen), for the Believer; we can see His effects in shaping and forming the Image of Christ on the cast of our Heart. Neither the Heat, Light nor the Chemical effect of the Sun is the Sun; all three make the Sun, each performing a separate work. Thus, the Father, Son and Holy Spirit are God; and they in their united ability are God; each performing His official work of preserving the Universe.

A closer look at other Scriptures reveals the unity of the Godhead. During His earthly ministry, Christ's mission included, among other things, revealing the other members of the Trinity. He said, "For I have come down from heaven to do the Will of God Who sent Me, not to do what I want. And this is the Will of God, that I should not lose even one of all those He has given Me, but that I should raise them to eternal life at the last day." [7]

Many things that He said revealed the Father and Holy Spirit, such as, "And I will ask the Father, and He will give you another Counselor to be with you forever—".[8] In another passage He says, "But the Counselor, the Holy Spirit, Whom the Father will send in My name, will teach you all things and will remind you of everything I have said to you."[9] Or, "When the Counselor comes, Whom I will send to you from the Father, the Spirit of Truth Who goes out from the Father, He will testify about Me."[10] These all speak of the Spirit proceeding from the Father and, sent by both the Father and the Son, to testify of the works of Christ.

But there are other Scriptures in the Old Testament, which also give hints of the Trinity, for example, "Come near Me and listen to this: 'From the first announcement I have not spoken in secret; at the time it happens, I Am there.' And now the Sovereign LORD has sent Me, with His Spirit."[11] Or, "So he said to me, 'This is the Word of the LORD to Zerubbabel: "Not by might nor by power, but by My Spirit," says the LORD Almighty.'"[12]

The New Testament clarifies this further. Paul saying, "There is One Body, and One Spirit, just as you were called in One Hope of your calling; One LORD, One Faith, One Baptism, One God and Father of all, Who is above all, and through all, and in you all."[13] "For there is One God, and One mediator between God and men, the man Christ Jesus."[14]

ೞ⬥ೞ THE FATHER ⬥ೞ⬥

The Father holds the place of Headship and is the Presenter of the Master Plan of Creation and Redemption.

The Scriptures declare that "God is Love," and He has shown us His Love, He chose us, He picked us out for Himself as His Own in Christ BEFORE the Creation and, the Foundation of the world. He planned that we should be holy and blameless in His sight, even above reproach, before Him in LOVE. For He Foreordained, Predestined us, and Planned in love for adoption as His own children through Jesus Christ. This He did by the good pleasure of His Will so that we might be to the praise and the commendation of His glorious Grace. Grace that He has so freely given to us In the Beloved, the One He Loves. In Him, we have redemption, deliverance, and salvation through His blood, the remission, and forgiveness of sins, offenses, shortcomings, and trespasses. This He did by the riches of God's gracious favor, which He lavished upon us with all wisdom and understanding, practical insight and

> "HE CHOSE US, HE PICKED US OUT FOR HIMSELF AS HIS OWN IN CHRIST BEFORE THE CREATION AND, THE FOUNDATION OF THE WORLD."

prudence. He did this by making known to us the mystery, the secret of His Will of His Plan, and of His Purpose. This He did according to His good pleasure, His merciful intention, which He Purposed in Christ.

He planned this to be put into effect when the times reached their fulfillment. At the maturity of the times and at the climax of the Ages—to bring all things in Heaven and on Earth together unifying and consummating all things under One Head, even Christ. In Him we were also chosen, made God's heritage and part, heirs having obtained an inheritance; *for we had been predestined, foreordained, chosen and appointed beforehand.*

All this according to and by THE PLAN of Him Who works out everything in agreement with and conformity to the Purpose the Counsel and Design of His Own WILL. So that we who first hoped in Christ, who first put our confidence in Him have been destined and appointed to live for the praise of His glory!"[15] He did this that He might clearly demonstrate in and through The Ages to come the incomparable immeasurable, limitless, surpassing riches of His free grace, expressed in His kindness toward us in Christ Jesus.[16]

Throughout the Scripture's we find many precious gems of truth about God's Love, who He is, what He has done, and the many yet unfulfilled things that He is carrying to their conclusion, *as He fulfills His Master Plan.* All of this done "according to the terms of the *Eternal and Timeless Purpose* which *He realized and carried into effect in the person of Christ Jesus our Lord.*"[17]

God the Father is head over all. God the Father Created All Matter. 1 Corinthians 8:6a, states, "For us there is but one God, the Father, from Whom All things came and for Whom we live. While the AMP says, "Yet for us there is only One God, the Father, Who is the Source of All things and for Whom we have life.

The Father is the Source of everything that exists, He brought all things into existence, He is the source of all. He begot the Son. God the Son formed and shaped everything. 1Corinthians 8:6b, states, "And there is but one LORD, Jesus Christ, through Whom All things came and through Whom we live. While the AMP says, "And One Lord, Jesus Christ, through and by Whom are All things and through and by Whom we ourselves exist.

The Son, "the Word," took and formed all matter, spiritual and physical, into its various shapes and forms the Holy Spirit as the "Breath of God" gave life to those forms that have life.

In the Old Testament, it was the work and intervention of the Father, the Word, and the Holy Spirit, laying the foundation of this phase of the

Plan. Then, the "Pre-Carnate" Christ, as representative of the Godhead, revealed Himself to men in many and varied disguises. Then, the Holy Spirit came upon men, empowering them to do specific works of God, and then left them. We see the work of the Son during Christ's earthly ministry. He came, sent by the Father, as representative of the Godhead, He did everything the Father would have done, had He come, thus we see the Son, guided by the Holy Spirit, doing the Father's Will. He would complete the Plan in the Cross. Therefore, we can see God's presence always with us, with anyone of the persons of the Godhead at work, the work varying according to the seasons of the Plan.

This present dispensation reveals the work of the Holy Spirit as Restrainer of the worlds "anti-Christian spirit of lawlessness," while He separates "the Church" out of the world.[18] Remember Jesus said, "I will never leave or abandon you, and that He would not leave us orphans." He said, "if I go away, I will send you a Comforter; He will remain with you forever," and this we know to be true, "for now we see God with us, in the person of the Holy Spirit." [19]

From the beginning, the Father, Son, and Holy Spirit have been actively working to fulfill the Master's Plan of Salvation, Redeeming the Creation. Thus, we have God's Love revealed in, and through, the work of the three persons of the Godhead: the Father, Son, and Holy Spirit.

ෲ THE SON (THE WORD) ෲ

The Son carries out the Representative duties of the Master's Plan. He is our Advocate with the Father in the Master Plan of Creation and Redemption.[20]

Jesus said, "Not that anyone has ever seen the Father; only I, Who was *sent* from God, have seen Him."[21] "No one has seen God (the Father) at any time. The only begotten Son, who is in the bosom of the Father, He has declared Him." [22]

The Scripture says, "Christ is the visible image of the invisible God. He existed before God made anything at all and is supreme over all Creation. Christ is the One through Whom God created everything in heaven and earth. He made the things we can see and the things we cannot see—kings, kingdoms, rulers, and authorities. Everything has been created through Him and for Him. He existed before everything else began, and He holds all Creation together. Christ is the Head of the Church, which is His body. He is the first who will rise from the dead, so He is first in everything." [23]

The Son is the sole expression, the Light Being, the Divine out-raying or the radiance of God's Glory and the exact representation perfect imprint and very image and nature of His Being, sustaining upholding and supporting, guiding, and propelling the universe, and all things by His powerful Word, His mighty Word of power. After He had provided purification for sins, by offering Himself, carrying out our cleansing of sins and riddance of guilt, He sat down at the right hand of the Divine Majesty in Heaven on High.[24]

The Plan was and is a revelation of the, "I AM, the Alpha and Omega, the beginning and the end." [25] The One who's goings forth are from of old, from everlasting.[26] He is, "the Word of God, the Creator Revealer, and the Angel of the LORD."[27] Having existed from all eternity, He was from the beginning, "the Word," He is the Word, *"the Logos."* "In the beginning was the Word, the Word was with God, and the Word was God. He was in the Beginning with God." [28] He is at One in mind and purpose with the Father and the Holy Spirit, all of Whom have Life.

IT WAS CHRIST:

The Word restored the Earth back to an inhabitable state in Genesis 1:3-31, the Word said, "Let there be Light."[29] He formed all plant and animal creations out of the dust of the earth. He planted the Garden of Eden. He formed Adam in "His Image and Likeness," out of the dust of the earth, then breathed into his nostrils "the breath of life."[30] He once breathed on the disciples saying, "Receive the Holy Spirit."[31] He put the man whom He had formed in the Garden.[32]

It was His voice that they heard walking in the Garden in the cool of the day. He charged Adam and Eve with eating the fruit, from the forbidden tree.[33] He gave them the Promise, about "the Seed" of the woman.[34] He charged Cain with the murder of his brother Abel.[35]

He called Noah, warning him of the Flood, telling him to build an Ark.[36] He came down with the Father and the Holy Spirit to see the city and tower of Babel.[37]

He called (Abram) Abraham, from Ur of Chaldees, to go to Canaan.[38] "The Word" appeared several times to Abraham; He gave him "The Abrahamic Covenant."[39]

He appeared to Abraham in the plains of Mamre, "Abraham lifted his eyes and looked, and low, three Men stood by him." Abraham knew it was the Lord with two angels, in disguise. Abraham said, "Let water be fetched to wash your feet... He took butter, and milk, and the calf he had dressed and set it before Them, and They did eat." He foretold Abraham of the birth of Isaac, and afterward rebuked Sarah for laughing, and then denying that she laughed, He said, "Is anything to hard for the Lord?"

Afterward, they rose, and looked toward Sodom, and Abraham went with them to bring them on the way. The Lord said, "Because the cry of Sodom and Gomorrah is great, I will go down now and see." Abraham stood yet before the Lord and drew near to intercede for Sodom and Gomorrah. He interceded asking, "Would you destroy the righteous with the wicked?" Abraham bargained with the Lord from forty-five souls down to ten, in the end the Lord saying, "I will not destroy it for the sake of ten." Afterward the Lord went His way, and Abraham returned to his place. [40]

Isaac and Jacob saw him several times; He confirmed and reminded them of the Abrahamic Covenant. He, whose name was secret, wrestled with Jacob all night at the ford of Jabbok. There He touched the socket of Jacob's hip and afterward changed his name to Israel. On this bodily appearance of God, Jacob said, "I have seen God face to face, and my life is preserved."[41] Moses saw him in a flame of fire out of the midst of the Burning Bush, in the Wilderness.

He called to Moses twice and then he said, "I AM the God of your fathers, the God of Abraham, the God of Isaac, and the God of Jacob." At this, Moses hid his face, because he was afraid to look at God.[42]

When Moses said to God, "Suppose I go to the Israelites and say to them, 'The God of your fathers has sent me to you,' and they ask me, 'What is His name?' Then what shall I tell them?" God said to Moses, "I AM WHO I AM. {Or I WILL BE WHAT I WILL BE} This is what you are to say to the Israelites, 'I AM has sent me to you.'" God also said to Moses, "Say to the Israelites, 'The LORD, the God of your fathers—the God of Abraham, the God of Isaac, and the God of Jacob—has sent me to you.' This is My name forever, the name by which I Am to be remembered from generation to generation."[43] This is one of many instances in the Word where the record uses the phrase, "the Angel of the Lord" for God Himself.[44]

He sent ten great plagues upon Egypt,[45] and commanded the slaying of "the Passover Lamb," which was a "type" of Himself. [46] Through Moses, God instituted the Passover feast to atone for the sins of the people.[47] This was another representative "Type" of *the blood that covers.* The blood of the sacrificial lamb was to be applied on the doorpost and across the lintel of the doorway,[48] this formed a cross. Moses directed them to place the lamb sacrifice on a fire with one wooden stake driven through the length of its body, head to end to hold it on the fire. Another stake through the shoulders to turn it on the fire;[49] these stakes formed a cross. He told them not to break a bone.[50] The households of those who applied the blood ate the sacrificed lamb in Egypt; God spared their firstborn from death.[51]

As we said earlier about the principle of obedience, it is only through obedience and the shed blood of God's innocent lamb, His only Son, that we are, or can be, saved.[52] In type, this reminds us of the first lamb sacrificed, which He introduced to cover Adam and Eves nakedness and shame, replacing the fig leaves, clothing them with animal skins instead.[53] In a type this represented "the Blood sacrifice of a Lamb" to cover our sin. It reminds us of God's acceptance of Abel's offering, when he offered the blood sacrifice of the firstborn of his flock. In this God signaled the way of acceptability, Abel's sacrifice was one of substitution, Cains was one of Works.[54]

In type, we also think of God's testing of Abraham who in obedience, took and offered Isaac, his only begotten son, on Mount Mariah. The story of Abraham and Isaac is one of obedience and shows God willing to accept a sacrifice of innocence, but more importantly this pointed out God's Plan for an ultimate sacrifice.[55], it was Abraham's Faith and Obedience (because Abraham trusted and believed God), "that God accounted his Faith for Righteousness. (See Romans 4:13-25). Jesus Christ is the promised and perfect sacrifice for sin. He is the one that God spoke of, in the Garden, "as the Seed of the woman" who would bruise the head of the serpent. His life given to take away our sin and guilt before God, and as it was in Egypt, so it is for us today, everyone must apply the blood.[56]

Through taking in the Word of God, by faith we have the Life Blood of Jesus running over and washing away our sins, cleansing and renewing our hearts. For it is the shed Blood of Jesus Christ applied, that saves us, washes and cleanses us from all sin and unrighteousness.[57] John called Him, "the Lamb of God" saying, "Behold the Lamb of God which takes away the sin of the world."[58] It is by Faith that we Believe in the shed blood of Christ to remove our guilt and sin before God.

If only men taught these truths in our schools how
many of our children would be saved.

There is Life in the Blood; He died so you and I might live; He became poor so we might become rich. These are but a few of the "Types," the forerunners, representative of, "the Lamb of God, the Lamb of Calvary. In the Book of Revelation, we see Him standing before the Throne, as the

Lamb slain from the foundation of the World." [59] All of this confirms the Plan is about "Him."

He opened the Red sea and led Israel over across it on dry ground; He led them through the wilderness. He gave Moses the Ten Commandments. He gave him patterns and drawings to make the Tabernacle in the Wilderness, with all its coverings, furnishings, and utensils. He was told, "See to it that you make them according to the pattern which was shown you on the mountain." [60]

He fed Israel in the wilderness, "Manna," the bread from heaven, each of these are Old Testament "Types." He appeared in a visible body, to Joshua as Captain of the army of the Lord of Host, having a "sword drawn in His hand. Joshua asked, "Are you for us or against us." He received worship when "Joshua fell on his face to the earth and worshipped Him."[61] There were many more appearances of, "the Word" in the Old Testament. (We cover this in more detail in other volumes of this series).

Moses told Israel that, "The LORD your God will raise up for you a Prophet like me from your midst, from your brethren. Him you shall hear." [62] When it comes to the Will of God, God meant Jesus, the "Last Adam" to have many brothers and sisters. "And so, it is written, *The first man Adam became a living being.*" The last Adam *became* a life-giving spirit. However, the spiritual is not first, but the natural, and afterward the spiritual. The first man *was* of the earth, *made* of dust; the second Man *is* the Lord from heaven. As *was* the *man* of dust, so also *are* those *who are made* of dust; and as *is* the heavenly *Man,* so also *are* those *who are* heavenly. And as we have borne the image of the *man* of dust, we shall also bear the image of the heavenly *Man.*" [63]

"The Word became flesh and made His dwelling among us. We have seen His Glory, the Glory of the Only Begotten Who came from the Father, full of grace and truth." [64] This passage speaks of our Lord being the "only begotten" of the Father. He came to live among us as a man, having laid down His power, God prepared a body for Him that He might come and live with us in the form of a man.[65] He came into the world the same way as every other man.

> "THE WORD BECAME FLESH AND MADE HIS DWELLING AMONG US. WE HAVE SEEN HIS GLORY, THE GLORY OF THE ONLY BEGOTTEN WHO CAME FROM THE FATHER, FULL OF GRACE AND TRUTH."

The Father sent Him. While Christ was on earth, the Father, through the Holy Spirit, worked in and through His Son. In the following, Jesus challenges all teachings of there being many ways or paths leading to God. He said, "Do not let your HEARTS be troubled. Trust in God; trust also in Me. In My FATHER'S house are many rooms; if it were not so, I would have told you. I AM going there to PREPARE a place for you. And if I go and PREPARE a place for you, I will come back and take you to be with Me that you also may be where I AM. You know the WAY to the place where I AM going." Thomas said to Him, "Lord, we don't know where You are going, so how can we know the WAY?"

Jesus answered, "I AM the WAY and the TRUTH and the LIFE. *No one comes to the FATHER except through Me.*" [66]
When He asked the Disciples who do men say that I Am, they mentioned several names, He then said to them, but who do you say that I Am. Simon Peter answered, "You are the Christ, {Or Messiah} the Son of the LIVING God.67

In the New Testament the *"I AM"* revealed Himself saying, *I AM* "the Bread of Life."[68] He is the true Bread, the "Manna" from Heaven; the One Who satisfies the hunger and thirst of all who seek Eternal Life. *I AM* "the Light of the World."[69] He is the One Who brought light into this dark world, for although we walk through the wilderness of this world we don't have to walk in darkness, for in Him we have "the Light of Life." *I AM* "the Door of the sheep."[70] He is the One Who gathers the sheep; they know His voice and follow Him. They refuse to follow the voices of thieves and robbers, who would steal kill and destroy them. He is "the True Shepherd." *I AM* "the Good Shepherd."[71] He keeps His sheep; He watches over, protects, and cares for them. *I AM* "the Resurrection and the Life."[72] He will raise and give Eternal Life to His people. When He returns at "the Rapture" for His Church, He will be "the resurrection" for those who have died, and "the life" for those who have not. *I AM* "the Way, the Truth and the Life."[73] He is the only *Way* to the Father, He is the *Truth*, revealing God, He came to communicate to the spiritually dead, the *Life* of God. *I AM* "the True Vine."[74] He is the One Who came to fulfill God's Plan. Together as we, the branches, abide in Him, and He (the Vine) abides in us, we produce fruit, fruit that pleases God, fruit that honor God, when His life flows in and through ours.

In Him was Life, and that Life was the Light of Men.[75]

The Apostle Peter declares that "God chose Him for this purpose *long before the world began*, but now in these final days, He was sent to the earth for all to see. And He did this for you."[76]

The Apostles Peter, James, and John were eyewitnesses of His Majesty, when they saw His transfiguration on the mount of transfiguration.[77]

John wrote, "And the Word (Christ) became flesh (human, incarnate) and tabernacled (fixed His tent of flesh, lived awhile) among us; and we *actually* saw His glory (His honor, His majesty), such glory as an only begotten Son receives from His Father, full of grace (favor, loving-kindness) and truth."[78] Peter later wrote, "For we were not making up clever stories when we told you about the power of our Lord Jesus Christ and His Coming Again. We have seen His majestic splendor with our own eyes. And He received honor and glory from God the Father when God's glorious, majestic voice called down from heaven, 'This is My beloved Son; I am fully pleased with Him.' We ourselves heard the voice when we were there with Him on the holy mountain."[79]

The Father sent His Son so men might know what the Father is like. Christ is the One "Who was crucified on the Cross for our sins, He personally carried our sins away in His own body on the Cross so we can become dead to sin and live for what is right. You have been healed by His wounds!"[80] After being nailed to the Cross, before He died, He declared, "It is Finished." After His Resurrection, having given His disciples the Good News of the Kingdom, He gave them the Great Commission, the charge to continue to present God's "Plan of Salvation" to men. Having appointed the eleven to meet Him in Galilee, at the mountain, Jesus came and spoke to them saying:

"Go therefore, and make disciples of All the Nations, Baptizing them in the name of the Father, and of the Son, and of the Holy Ghost: teaching them to observe All Things that I have commanded you: And, lo, I Am with you always, even to the end of the Age. Amen."[81]

When Jesus gave His disciples "the Great Commission" to preach "the Good News" of the Gospel to every nation and every creature, this was the Good News God wanted shared with the entire world, even today.

What was Jesus Mission? – We cover this in Chapter 8,
"The Purpose of the Plan," and Chapter 14, "Lord Open our Eyes."

While the Father is the Presenter, the Son the Representative, as we have seen the Holy Spirit, the third person of the Godhead is the Revealer. Jesus in the beginning commanded His disciples to wait until they were imbued with power from on high. That power, "the Holy Spirit," was the promised Counselor.

⊰⊱⊰ THE HOLY SPIRIT ⊱⊰⊱

The Holy Spirit holds the place of Comforter, Counselor and is the Revealer of the Master Plan of Creation and Redemption.[82]

It was at Pentecost that He appeared as a mighty rushing wind from heaven and settled on the heads of the disciples in the upper room. Anointing them with power, He caused them to speak in other tongues; languages they had not previously learned, which is like what He did at the "Tower of Babel."[83]

Anointed by the Holy Spirit, they ministered to many who had made the journey from many other parts of the world to Jerusalem to keep "the Passover." Amazed and perplexed by the event, the people asked, "What does all of this mean?"[84] Peter stood up and explained, and from this event we see the beginnings of the Church. On that day, over 3,000 came to Christ. [85] Many visiting Jerusalem to keep the Passover became witnesses, and, no doubt, the Spirit caused them to carry accounts of the "Good News, He is Risen," back to their home countries. For us the empty tomb, the resurrection, and the outpoured Holy Spirit revealed the Father's acceptance of Christ's sacrifice on the cross. Now we see the person and work of the Holy Spirit carrying the Plan forward, under direction of the Father and the Son. His work is to reveal "The Plan." He inspired men to write out the Plan and has strived with them during the different administrations (dispensations) of God's purpose. He framed God's dealings with men on the earth. It was the risen, glorified Christ, "The Lamb of God," the sacrifice for our sins, who before leaving the earth introduced His disciples to the Ministry of the Comforter. In John 16:7-11 Jesus said, "Nevertheless I tell you the truth. It is to your advantage that I go away; for if I do not go away, the Helper (Holy Spirit) will not come to you; but if I leave, I will send Him to you. And when He has come, He will convict the world of sin, and of righteousness, and of judgment: of sin, because they do not believe in Me; of righteousness, because I go to My Father and you see Me no more; of judgment, because the ruler of this world is judged.

> "NEVERTHELESS, I TELL YOU THE TRUTH. IT IS TO YOUR ADVANTAGE THAT I GO AWAY; FOR IF I DO NOT GO AWAY, THE HELPER (HOLY SPIRIT) WILL NOT COME TO YOU; BUT IF I DEPART, I WILL SEND HIM TO YOU. AND WHEN HE HAS COME, HE WILL CONVICT THE WORLD OF SIN, AND OF RIGHTEOUSNESS, AND OF JUDGMENT:"

Of sin, Jesus said, "Because they do not believe in Me." Here the sin is not breaking one of the Ten Commandments which say, "you shall not, steal, kill or commit adultery." No, it is the sin of unbelief, the sin of rejecting Christ as the Savior of the world, rejecting "the Promise" made to Eve in the Garden, of the "Promised Seed," who had finally come. It is the work of the Spirit, convicting man of Sin, whenever the Message, "the Good News" of Salvation, is preached.

Of righteousness, "Jesus said, 'Because I go to My Father and you see Me no more.'" He convicts the world of sin, and the need for righteousness. The Creation is still under a curse; the Holy Spirit perpetuates the Message of Righteousness and convinces men that full pardon is available for all who will receive Him. The empty tomb displayed the Father's satisfaction with Christ's sacrifice, the penalty for sin paid in full. He reveals Christ's righteousness to the chosen, "the whosoever wills," those who the Father knew and picked out for Himself, even before the beginning of the world.

Believing in, and receiving, Christ's sacrifice for our sin is the test that men must pass in this present age to receive the gift of everlasting life.

Of judgment, "Jesus said, 'Because the ruler of this world is judged.'" After the fall, "Sin," which is a principle of Satan, ruled over the hearts of unregenerate man. The death of Adam and Eve's spirit was a reality. Having eaten of the fruit of the tree of knowledge of good and evil, man lost God consciousness; spiritually he went from innocence to death, God said, "In the day you eat of it, you shall surely die."[86]

Spiritually dead, his mind became blind and ignorant to the truth, which opens fellowship with God. Yet in each generation there has been a remnant with hope,[87] their spirit rekindled by God, who kept "the Hope of Salvation"[88] alive. These people looked and waited for "the Coming Messiah." "The Old Testament Saints looked forward to the First Coming, the New Testament Saints the Second." It was at the Cross, at Christ first coming (in fulfillment of the Promise), that Satan stood judged. It is the role of the Holy Spirit to convince men that "the author of Sin," the prince of this world, now stands condemned.[89] Christ will carry out this judgment at His Second Coming.[90]

WHERE DO YOU STAND?

Now to convict means "to convince" or "reprove" through the witness and testimony of another. Sin means "to miss the mark," to fall short of God's Purpose.[91] Now, a person is either a child of God, or a child of the Devil (the Enemy). Either people will stand for God or fall with Satan; there is no middle ground. All who side with Satan (the Accuser), having rejected God's Plan, will take part in his judgment.

Before leaving to heaven Jesus told His disciples, "I have much more to say to you, more than you can now bear. But when He, the Spirit of Truth, comes, He will guide you into all Truth. He will not speak on His own; He will speak only what He hears, and *He Will Tell You What Is Yet To Come.* He will bring Glory to Me by taking from what is Mine and making it known to you. All that belongs to the Father is Mine. That is why I said the Spirit will take from what is Mine and make it known to you."[92]

For those who will listen, the Spirit is doing this "Right Now."
The work of the Holy Spirit is all too obvious when we see the millions of
lives over the course of history changed by His work.

CHAPTER 6

Foreknowledge

For whom He did Foreknow, He also did Predestinate to be Conformed to the Image of His Son, that He might be the Firstborn among many Brethren.[1]

In his first letter to the Church, inspired by the Holy Spirit, the Apostle Peter addressed his letter to God's *Elect*, to those whom he called strangers in the world, Chosen according to the Foreknowledge of God the Father. Those Chosen long ago, and made holy by the Spirit, because they obeyed Jesus Christ, and are cleansed by His Blood, He said, "Grace and peace be yours in abundance."[2]

There is a place in the mind of God, where Election and Foreknowledge meet. The word "Foreknowledge" *means* to foreknow, know before; in other words, this is God's knowledge of people and events before they happen. The Father foresaw, and foreknew everything, before it happened in Creation. Scripture abounds with examples of God's foreknowledge; case in point, "consider the subject of Prophecy." Prophecy is God, through foreknowledge, revealing the future. "Thus says the LORD, the King of Israel, and His Redeemer, the LORD of Host: I AM the First and I AM the Last; besides Me there is no God. Who is like Me? Let him stand and proclaim it, declare it, and set his proofs in order before Me, since I made and established the people of antiquity. Who has announced from of old the things that are coming? Then let them declare yet future things. Fear not, nor be afraid in the coming violent upheavals; have I not told you from of

> "THERE IS A PLACE IN THE MIND OF GOD, WHERE ELECTION AND FOREKNOWLEDGE MEET."

old and declared it? And you are My witnesses! Is there a God besides Me? There is no other Rock; I know not any."[3]

FOREKNOWLEDGE: REVELATIONS FROM GOD

The Word has given us a new knowledge of GOD. To the would-be fortune-tellers, astrologers and forecasters of the future and the times of the end, God says, "Declare what is to be, present it—let them take counsel together. Who foretold this long ago, Who declared it from the distant past? Was it not I, the LORD? And there is no God apart from Me, a Righteous God and a Savior; there is none but Me."[4] Throughout the Scriptures, God repeatedly reveals foreknowledge, it was the Master's Plan to not only make known countless events that have already come to pass, but by His Spirit, He would have us consider the ones that have not. By revelation, God chose to reveal many things to man, such as the beginning of Creation, the fall of man in the garden, His Plan of Redemption. In His Word, God revealed and preserved knowledge of events that would herald the end of this Age, and the future beyond. In fact, it is both Jew and Gentile (the circumcised and uncircumcised heathen) together, who form and make up His new creation called "the Church." [5] You would think that something this wonderful would-be common knowledge. However, the truth is, the Deceivers and the deceived, those who oppose the Plan, do not want it known. God has revealed all of this in His Word. *He opens our understanding; the Lord Himself opens the eyes and understanding of those who in sincerity seek out the truth, those who want to know.* Truth is we were predestined to salvation, according to the foreknowledge of our God and Father through the work of our Lord and Savior Jesus Christ. From eternity past, God knew all who would eventually accept, and those who would forever reject the offer of deliverance. Again, we are talking about the deliverance provided for those who have "Faith in His Son, the Lord Jesus Christ," those whose names God wrote in the Lamb's book of Life.[6] The Elect, those who enter the kingdom of Heaven, the glorious kingdom of the Next Age, and from there live on in Eternity, "the Called, the chosen and faithful" who will never forget, that He first chose us. [7]

Because He is the LORD God, we can say with confidence,
that He has known all His Works and Plans, Ages in advance.

Turning to the big picture, again, because He is Omniscient, the Alpha and Omega, the Beginning, and the End; He knows everything that happened —in the eternal past, the unfolding present, and the eternal future. For example, consider what we would recognize as four trillion years from now. Not only does He know everything going on throughout His Creation, but He also knows it intimately, which is something finite minds have a tough time grasping. He is already there. Stop, think for a moment, how and why you think He inspired men to write the Bible, the book that tells the story of our future. It is not that God must manipulate events to fulfill His prophetic word, on the contrary. The God Who, not bound by time, has seen and already knows the outcome. He is the God of right now, and it does not matter when right now is. He was there almost two thousand years ago, when our Savior hung on the Cross and died for the sin of the entire world. He will be there two thousand years from now when the whole Creation stands on the other side of the Millennial Kingdom. He has enabled man to grasp this idea of foreknowledge, through the witness of fulfilled Prophecy. Prophecy is for the benefit of man, and when properly understood shows the Sovereign God revealing by His Spirit, as fact to us, some past or future otherwise unknowable event. God's foreknowledge has made the Scriptures relevant for all-time.

GOD LAID THE FOUNDATION BEFORE CREATION

Jesus said to them, "Have you never read in the Scriptures: The very stone which the builders rejected and threw away HAS BECOME *the Cornerstone*; this is the LORD's doing, and it is marvelous in our eyes?[8] (See Psalm 118:22, 23). Christ is the foundation stone of the new kingdom; *He is the Rock.* (See Daniel 2:28-45). God the Father foreknew everyone who would see the Plan of Grace and Salvation, understand it, choose His Son, and have the faith to believe in Him, through the work of the Holy Spirit. The Father knew those to whom He would choose to reveal Himself; He foreknew everyone written in the lamb's book of life. He foreknew the men and women who would run the race, and with patience share the Message of the Kingdom with others. God wants to save all people for, "the Lord is not slack concerning *His* promise, as some count slackness, but is longsuffering toward us, not willing that any should perish but that all should come to repentance."[9]

While the offer of the Kingdom is a genuine offer made to the whosoever wills, God does not force it on any one of us. This does not mean that He did not know, for He foreknew all who would accept and who would reject the Plan. He foreknew everyone who would come to trust in, and claim, the promise, "those willing to let go of what we can't hold on to, to gain, what we can't lose."[10] He foreknew all who would walk in and grow the fruit of the Spirit, those rich in heart storing treasures in heavenly accounts,[11] the pilgrims, and strangers in this Age seeking a new home, "a mansion in heaven."[12]

He also foreknew all who would believe the lie, reject "the Message" and oppose the Plan, those whose names were not in (blotted out of), the Lamb's book of life.[13] The God of His Word always has both our present and future in mind. "And we know that in all things God works for the good of those who love Him, for God works with those who love Him, to bring about what is good." The Apostle Paul wrote, "And we know that all things work together for good to those who love God who have been called according to His purpose." For those whom He foreknew, He also predestined to be conformed to the likeness of His Son, that He might be the firstborn among many brothers. And those He predestined, He also called; those He called, He also justified; those He justified, He also glorified.[14] Through foreknowledge, God foresaw those who would wrap their hope in His promise, even the many who lived and died before He came. In His eyes, this was all a done deal. For while as a nation, unbelieving Israel rejected Jesus as "the Messiah," and many Jews still waiting for His first coming, the Church is waiting for His second. It is obvious now from the Scriptures, that God foresaw all of this.

> *"The God of Eternity, not bound by time,*
> *knows and declares the End from the Beginning."*

He is the God Who sees;[15] He is "the God Who is the same yesterday, today, and forever."[16] He saw our past—where we were, our present—as we are right now, and our future —as we will one day be. He is the One whose habitation is eternity.[17] From our birth until our death, He knows all the intimate details about us, not only our todays, but also our tomorrows, for He is already there. He knows when a sparrow falls or even a tree in the forest for that matter. Having created all the stars, He knows them all by name. Go out on a starlit night and "Lift your eyes and look to the heavens: Who created all these? He brings out the starry host one by one and calls them each by name. Because of His great power and mighty strength, not one of them is missing."[18] While you might feel insignificant, He is interested in you.

The mind of God is simultaneously aware of all things going on in Creation. God knows everything that has ever happened in Creation, and everything that ever will. God says, "For as the heavens are higher than the earth, so are My ways higher than your ways, And My thoughts than your thoughts."[19]

God's is a multidimensional view of all things, a multiple view of all events taking place in time. The Spirit of God, searching the Mind of God, has access to all knowledge, knowledge that transcends time. For example, by taking a closer look at Prophecy we get a snapshot of the Plan, and the many things going on in it over time. For example, let us look at Isaiah's writings; through Isaiah, the Spirit of God has given us a record of events, which will take place during the Millennium. Chapters 2, 4, 11, 14, 32, 35, 65 of Isaiah give in advance accounts of events, which will occur during the Millennium, the 1,000-year reign of Christ on the earth, even though from our perspective the Millennium has not happened yet. The Holy Spirit searches the mind of God and reveals secrets and mysteries in the mind of God about things past, present, or future. He reveals the Father's will to you. Even the things that

> "GOD'S IS A MULTIDIMENSIONAL VIEW OF ALL THINGS, A MULTIPLE VIEW OF ALL EVENTS TAKING PLACE IN TIME. THE SPIRIT OF GOD, SEARCHING THE MIND OF GOD, HAS ACCESS TO ALL KNOWLEDGE, KNOWLEDGE THAT TRANSCENDS TIME."

we may have forgotten, the Holy Spirit is able to bring to our remembrance and understanding. Just as the Spirit of God searches the mind of God, revealing the LORD's Will to us, He searches to know what is in the heart of a man. "The spirit of a man is the lamp of the LORD, searching all the inner depths of his heart."[20] By nature, man looks at the outer appearance; man bases his judgments, opinions, and assumptions about others solely on what he sees. But God does not look at man's physical appearance or stature, God looks at the heart, "For the LORD does not see as man sees; for man looks at the outward appearance, but the LORD looks at the heart."[21]

We should ask for the wisdom to see ourselves as He sees us.

The LORD knows and sees the souls of all, both good and evil, those who embrace, and those who have rejected His Son. Knowing this can and should be a staggering thought when you consider the implications. Remember,

"The eyes of the LORD run to and fro throughout the whole earth, to show Himself strong on behalf of those whose heart is loyal toward Him."[22]

Aren't you glad you know Him? The last words that anyone of us would want to hear Him say are, "Depart from Me for I never knew you."[23] Knowing all of this should give us strong incentive to cooperate with Him in fulfilling, "The Vision of Faith" that He has for our lives. He is with us, all the way, to help us fulfill our purpose and destiny while here on the earth. Can you now see how our Prayers of Faith have the power to influence His Plan? Prayer is the way that we have access to and influence with the Father.[24] By prayer, we can affect both His Will and the Plan. When we know His Will and Plan, we can ask "according to His Will" and receive the things we ask, because the Father gives us what we need. It strengthens our hope when we know that He knows everything about us, and yet, He still loves us, He sees us as we are and yet has Faith-Vision for each one of us. His foreknowledge see's us not only where we are, but also as we will be at the end of our journey, "Righteous and in right standing before Him."[25] Anyone familiar with the Psalms has seen among them

> "HE'S WITH US, ALL THE WAY, TO HELP US FULFILL OUR PURPOSE AND DESTINY WHILE HERE ON THE EARTH.

the many gems, which unveil incredible insight that help us understand the personal qualities of our God and Father, and the depths of His love for us. We try to remind you of this, throughout this work.

"DIVINE APPOINTMENTS"

With everything said, when you began your search to know the truth, you may have soon discovered there were obvious and yet undeniable events taking place in your life. Some call these fate, others chance or coincidence; Believers call them *"Divine Appointments."* By "Divine Appointment," spiritually, you can feel and sense the Father guiding your life, through the work of the Spirit. Think about it, in your times of study and meditation on His Word, have you ever felt His presence guiding you to the Truth, just as Jesus said He would?

This is all part of His faith affirming witness to us. Divine interventions occur throughout the Bible, each showing a pattern of His providence, and through seeing them, we learn to trust in His faithfulness. This is where the God of the Bible becomes personal and real, real to our heart and mind. Look at your own life, can you think of an experience where everything just clicked, things just came together and fell in place. Those moments that you could not have planned better, even if you tried, those moments that you somehow knew you were in the right place at the right time. You knew that you were right where you needed to be in the center of His Will. Could it be that even you picking up and reading this book is another act of Divine Providence, and somewhere in these pages is a Message from God, just for you? His Plans for you are more real than you think. Divine Appointments are appointments in time, which lead us on to our eternal destiny.

These "Divine Appointments" are milestones, key events, which mark the climax, the beginning, or end of a life chapter in our already authored book in heaven. They come to us from the hands of a Sovereign God and loving Father; He appoints them; they are comparable to street signs; they occur throughout our lives. They give hope and direction, information (confirmation if you will); they guide and direct us through this life to our journey's end. These are confirmations, which let us know He is still there, that He has not left nor will He abandon us.[26] There are many examples in the Plan of His hand of providence.[27] We find them expressed in and through the lives of the saints, many times appearing at a low point in their lives, at their wits end, having done all they could do, then "suddenly," God turns everything around. Look at the lives of Old Testament saints; look at the summary of lives in Hebrews Hall of Faith. (See Hebrews Chapter 11). Look at the life of Jesus, and the lives of the New Testament saints. Throughout the Word, we see things occurring at *appointed times.* Look at the lives of people you know; think about your own life. The Father wants us to learn from the examples given in His Word and come out in victory over as many of these appointments as possible. Listen, have you heard "His still small voice;"[28] do you hear, understand, and heed His warnings, do you realize when confronted with a "Divinely appointed, life changing event."

When we take note of and follow His lead, we are *walking in the Spirit and not after the flesh.*[29] We have the hope and testimony of the many that have gone before us. They declare that He is Faithful.[30] They themselves kept their appointed dates with destiny, their own "Divine Appointments," through obedience; they fulfilled Gods calling on their lives. Many stood against overwhelming circumstances, yet they chose to obey God, thus fulfilling their purpose, and His Will. *"How about you?"*

Part 3 –

"Knowing the Plan"

CHAPTER 7

Rightly Dividing the Word

Study to show yourself approved of God, a workman who does not have need to be ashamed, rightly dividing the Word of Truth.[1]

THE BIBLE: OUR REGULATION AND TRAINING MANUAL

As "the Owner's Manual," the Bible holds all the information and instruction that a child of God will ever need to know His Plan, as noted in this tribute to the Word of God.

"The Bible is not an amulet, a charm, a fetish, or a book that will work wonders by Its presence. However, It is a Book that will work wonders in every life, here and from now on, if acted on and obeyed in faith and sincerity. Its revelation of the origin and destiny of all things, God inspired. Written in the simplest human language possible It is translatable into any language, so the most unlearned can understand and obey Its teachings. It is self-interpreting and covers every subject of human knowledge and need, now and forever. As a literary composition, the Bible is the most remarkable Book ever written. It is a Divine library of 66 books, some of notable size, others no larger than a tract. These Books include various forms of Literature, History, Biographies, Poetry, Proverbial sayings, Hymns, Letters, directions for elaborate Ritualistic Worship, Laws, Parables, Riddles, Allegories, Secrets, Mysteries, Prophecy, Drama, embracing all manner of literary styles in human expression. The Book reveals the mind of God, the state of man, the way of Salvation, the doom of Sinners, and the happiness of Believers. Its Doctrines are holy, Its precepts binding, Its histories true, and Its decisions immutable.

> "THE BOOK REVEALS THE MIND OF GOD, THE STATE OF MAN, THE WAY OF SALVATION, THE DOOM OF SINNERS, AND THE HAPPINESS OF BELIEVERS."

Read It to be wise, believe It to be safe, and practice It to be holy. The Bible has light to direct you, food to support you, and comfort to cheer you. It is the travelers map, the pilgrim's staff, the pilot's compass, the soldier's sword, and the Christian's charter. Here the way to heaven stands open, and the gates of hell shown. Christ is Its grand subject; our good is Its design, and the glory of God Its end. It should fill your memory, rule your heart, and guide your feet in righteousness and true holiness. Read It slowly, often, prayerfully, meditatively, searchingly, devotionally, and study It constantly, perseveringly, and industriously. Read It until It becomes part of your being and produces faith that will move mountains. The Bible is a mine of wealth, the source of health, and a world of pleasure. Given to you in this life, and opened at the judgment, It will stand forever. It involves the highest responsibilities, will reward the least to the greatest effort to understand It, and will condemn all who trifle with Its sacred contents."

Author: *Unknown*.

RIGHTLY DIVIDING THE WORD

Now God gave the Bible to man through men. The various parts of Scripture came by His audible voice, inspiration, revelations, visions and dreams, angels, prophets, apostles, and the Lord Jesus "Himself." In a word, the Master Plan unveils and reveals His-Story, written in advance. Throughout the Bible, God allowed His people to undergo trials and tests to reveal and let us see their heart. He recorded their accounts for our learning and instruction, His intent was for us to study His Word, discover the truths, learn from them, and grow and mature from the experiences of past generations.

> *The Law of the Lord is perfect, restoring the whole person;*
> *The Testimony of the Lord is sure, making wise the simple.*
> *The Precepts of the Lord are right, rejoicing the heart;*
> *The Commandment of the Lord is pure and bright, enlightening the eyes.*
> *The Reverent Fear of the Lord is clean, enduring forever;*
> *The Ordinances of the Lord are true and righteous altogether.*
> *More to be desired are they than gold, even than much fine gold; they are*
> *   sweeter also than honey and drippings from the honeycomb.*
> *Moreover, by them is Your servant warned (reminded, illuminated, and*
> *   instructed); and in keeping them there is great reward.*

Who can discern his lapses and errors? Clear me from hidden and unconscious faults.

Keep back Your servant also from presumptuous sins; let them not have dominion over me! Then shall I be blameless, and I shall be innocent and clear of great transgression.

Let the words of my mouth and the meditation of my heart be acceptable in Your sight, O Lord, my firm, impenetrable Rock and my Redeemer.2

Be diligent and eager, do your utmost to show yourself approved of God, you are His workmanship, you have no need or cause to be ashamed, as you correctly analyze, accurately divide, rightly handle, and skillfully teach the Word of Truth.[3]

Pick a place in the Bible, now pick a person and you will find God revealing His perspective on a historical event. The Word provides examples, teachings, admonitions, and instructions for all who want to get it right. It is our source of God's revelation of wisdom, truth, knowledge, understanding, and Prophecy. It has the many things the Father wanted revealed, to prepare us, His children, for the journey through this life. God gave His Word to equip us, "for the good works that He has committed to us." "Every Scripture is God-breathed, given by His inspiration. The teachings in His Word are profitable for instruction, for reproof and conviction of sin, for correction of error and discipline in obedience, *and* for training in righteousness. The kind of holy living, which brings us into conformity with God's Will in thought, purpose, and action, so that the man of God may be complete and proficient, well fitted and thoroughly equipped for every good work."[4]

Key Events. In the Word we see the Sovereign God revealing "Key events" in the lives of the main characters of the Scriptures. Starting with Adam, Eve, Cain, Abel, Noah, Nimrod, Abraham, Lot, Sarah, Hagar, Isaac, Jacob, Joseph, and his brothers, Moses and Pharaoh, Joshua, Gideon, David and Saul; the list goes on throughout the Old Testament and into the New. Beginning with the four Gospels, each one reveals "key events" in the life of Jesus Christ our Lord and Savior. The books, which follow, unveil the accounts of His disciples and witnesses chosen to spread the "Good News." God highlighted their lives for our example, teaching, and instruction. The Bible not only revealing key events in their lives, their conversations, their virtues, and many flaws; It also reveals what God wanted written in text and context. God did this in a way that ties the Old Testament to the New. Combining the books, God has given us an outline of just how He Planned to bring it all together for us, revealing the Master's Plan unfolded and understood.

Themes. In It are themes on origins and outcomes, time and eternity, things physical and spiritual, people and personalities, beginnings and ends, places and events, life-and-death, principles and rules, ways and laws, testimonies, statutes, commands, judgments, and His Word.

Doctrines. We find Doctrines on the Trinity, God the Father, the Son and the Holy Spirit, Man, Heaven and Hell, The Word, The Nations, The Church, Sin and Salvation, Satan, Angels, Prophecy, Ages and Dispensations and Appointed Times and Seasons.

Contrasts. Unless you are a full-time student of the Word, some of this might have gone right over your head. Yet there is much more, such as Faith versus Works; Heaven versus Hell; Physical versus Spiritual; Truth versus Lies; Sin versus Righteousness; the Church versus the Kingdom; under Law versus under Grace. There are also types and shadows, secrets, mysteries, prophecies, parables, and examples, reproofs, correction, and teachings, all intended for our instruction. Paul says that in God's dealings with Israel that, "these things happened to them as examples and were written down as warnings for us, on whom the fulfillment of the Ages has come.[5] The point is this; being "born again," you can understand "the Bible," God's Holy Word, just as you would any other book. To understand it, and "Rightly Divide the Word," you must know the "who, what, when, where, how and why." Read asking and answering the same questions you would have with any other book, with the understanding that God is going somewhere."

God, "the Holy Spirit," gave the Plan, line upon line, precept upon precept, here a little there a little. To understand it, you must connect the verses (dots) placing Scriptural events in there proper place and order. Think of the Plan as a puzzle, each new revelation adding a part to the whole, each revelation adding another piece (portion) to the Plan of Truth. Now imagine those portions with prophetic messages scattered out on a table, and you have a Prophetic puzzle of the Plan.

To see the whole Plan, our task is to take the prophecies and events revealed in the Old and New Testaments and place them in there proper place (right time and order of fulfillment). As you read this series of books on the Master Plan, you will see that this is what we have tried to do.

Jesus said, "You diligently study the Scriptures because you think that by them you have Eternal Life. These are the Scriptures that testify about Me"[6]

Now God gave the writings in the Old Testament, "from Genesis to Malachi," over a 1500-year period, while He had the New Testament books written in just under 50-years. Through progressive revelations, God was revealing Himself and the Plan with each new successive revelation, giving more light: the Prophets knew more than the Patriarch's and Judges, the New Testament Saints more than the Old.

The Old and New Testaments are not two separate books, the New Testament taking the place of the Old; they are half of a whole, and they are ONE. For we find the New Testament "enfolded" in the Old Testament and the Old Testament "unfolded" in the New. God hid the Master Plan in the Old Testament and revealed it in the New. Once more, to see the big picture we must, "Rightly divide the Word," placing the pieces and parts, in there proper place and order.

Of all the Old Testament, the Book of Genesis is the most hated and attacked by our enemy, for this book holds the accounts of *origins and beginnings*; without it, we would have no foundation for understanding the Plan. On the other hand, you cannot understand certain passages in the Old Testament without the revelations and clarifications given in the New. However, when you place Scriptures from both Old and New Testament books in order, you have a picture of "God's Master Plan."

All Scripture is given by inspiration of God, and is profitable for doctrine, for reproof, for correction, for instruction in Righteousness, that the man of God may be complete, thoroughly equipped for every good work.[7]

THE WORD: IN TEXT AND CONTEXT

To see the Plan clearly, we must keep the Biblical record "in context." For example, from God's perspective, it is clear the Bible divides humanity into three classes of people: the Jews, the Gentiles, and the Church. While the Bible is profitable to all classes of men, it is important to keep in mind its context, and just who the Scriptures are addressing. For some of its text apply specifically to the *Jew*, those who can trace their blood-lineage back to Abraham (the Old Testament text). Some to the *Gentile*, those who have no connection with Israel (the Jews), and have not come into the *Church*. Some to the Church, which consist of both Jews and Gentiles, who from "Pentecost to the Rapture" have come to confess, Jesus Christ as their personal Lord and Savior. Now just as it is true of His promises, God's purposes for each class are different. Just as the Jews would not try to claim a promise given to the Church, because some of the promises that apply to Israel do not apply to the Church. For in the Church, God is preparing a body for Christ in the Kingdom of Heaven. In Israel, God is preparing a kingdom on earth.

(A note here: there are some promises, which, with conditions met, God does not forbid men from laying claim to. We seek His Promises through prayer, by faith).

While God wrote the Bible for Israel and the Church, it is not just for Israel and the Church. Paul says that God wrote It for our example and learning, whether Jew, Gentile or Christian.[8] For example, the first chapters of Genesis (1 through 11) are profitable to all men. Here we have an account of the state and restoration of the earth, God's creation of man and woman, the fall, the flood, and the beginning of the nations. Starting with the call of Abram (Abraham) in Chapter 12, the rest of the Old Testament is a written history of God's dealing with the Jews, however again, the Bible's teachings, and lessons, are profitable for all classes of men. Like the Old, the New Testament writings address all of Creation but focus on consummating the Plan. In the New, we see God's final dealings with both spiritual and physical beings and all things in heaven and on earth, but it's focus is on God's disposition of Jews, Gentiles, and the Church. Now while the whole New Testament applies to the Church, the books of Hebrews and James address Jewish Christians. Another example of context would be "Romans Chapter 8," which is one of the greatest gems in the royal record; we note that its context reveals Paul writing *to* and *about* the Believer (the Church). Romans Chapters 9-11, written *to* the Church, not *about* the Church, but *about* Israel and God's setting the nation aside, while He formed His Church and all of this occurs during the *times of the Gentiles*.[9] (We discuss "the times of the Gentiles," in more detail, in other volumes of this work.). We Rightly Divide the Word when we take heed to whom the Bible is addressing. By doing so, we do not allegorize or spiritualize the Scriptures, which some do, when they try to apply Scriptures to a class of people the Holy Spirit never intended. Men do this when they take Scriptural promises written to the Jew (the nation Israel) and try to apply them to the Church. Again, Paul warned us that God wrote these things for our example, admonition and instruction.[10] We know that God is not the author of confusion,[11] therefore to see where the Plan is going, "We must rightly divide the Word."[12]

GOD IS BUILDING A KINGDOM

We see the Father as the Architect Designer, the Supplier of materials for the Plan. The Son as the Contractor Carpenter, the Commissioner of the builders in the Plan. The Holy Spirit is the Foreman, He is the conductor, orchestrating and directing men and the Church to carry out the various stages and events of the Plan. This He does as He hears and receives instruction from the Father and the Son. Creation is the stage, the background, and setting. This is God's house, built on Faith and Good Works.[13] These good works are the building materials out of which He is building the Church and the Kingdom. Satan and his followers look to hinder and block the progress of God's Plan and God's people. (See Nehemiah Chapters 4-6).

Jesus told His disciples, "Let not your heart be troubled; you believe in God, believe also in Me. In My Father's house are many mansions; if *it were* not *so,* I would have told you. *I go to prepare a place for you.* And if I go and prepare a place for you, I will come again and receive you to Myself; that where I Am, *there* you may be also.[14]

God created all things through "the Word." He is the One Who Created the Heavens and the Earth; He said to His disciples, "I go to prepare a place for you."

Here is another example of His foreknowledge. He went to prepare a place for each one of us, the members of His body, the Church. For Him to do this, He would have had to known in advance whom the mansions (houses) were for and based on our faithfulness and life's works, just how He would prepare each one of them. He would have to prepare them in a way that reflected and revealed our rewards of faithfulness while we were here on earth. The only surprises will be for those of us who came from earth. God has given us a preview of our future home in Revelations 21:1-22:5.

Another way to see the Plan is to consider it a guide for building two great works for the upcoming Age, "the Age to come." One part consists of a Kingdom on earth, fulfilling many Old Testament prophecies of a future earthly Kingdom, with Israel head of the nations. Meanwhile, God is preparing the Church for the Kingdom of Heaven; a spiritual family of redeemed and transformed children, a royal priesthood and holy nation; these are the saints who will rule and reign with Him.[15] Creation will realize both works in the Age to come. In the end, the Kingdom of God will consist of a living household of faith,[16] in which righteousness lives. Again, like a giant puzzle with all the periods and events placed in proper order, the Plan of God makes perfect sense. Thus, the student of the Word gains a new perspective and appreciation for the Will, Plan, and Purposes of our Father.

> "ANOTHER WAY TO SEE THE PLAN IS TO CONSIDER IT A GUIDE FOR BUILDING TWO GREAT WORKS FOR THE UP COMING AGE, "THE AGE TO COME.""

When we rightly divide the Word of Truth, what used to be fuzzy and confusing becomes clear. It is then the Master's Plan takes on a new meaning, and we realize that in Him, everything has a purpose, a beginning, and a predetermined end.

CHAPTER 8

The Purpose of the Plan

I have a Plan for the whole earth, for My Mighty Power reaches throughout the World."[1]

OUTLINE: "ANOTHER PICTURE OF THE ETERNAL PLAN"

As said earlier, the Master Plan included everything in Creation from beginning to end. This means everything in existence, in both the visible and invisible realms, spiritual and physical, all living and nonliving substances of matter, down to the smallest particle and tiniest microbe. God fixed the laws and rules, which governed the purpose for and existence of each. From the beginning, God was going somewhere, having both the beginning and end in mind. Before He restored the earth to the habitable state found in Genesis 1:3-2:4, God had a Plan. Before the beginning when one third of the angels followed Satan in rebellion against God, resulting in the destruction, which Genesis 1:2 reveals. Even before Genesis 1:1 when He called the universe into existence and created time, God had a Plan. All the way to end time events recorded in parts of the Old and New Testaments, events which point to the final destruction and renovation of the earth by fire, and a new heaven and earth.[2] We can see that God is taking us somewhere. As we study the Word, the Holy Spirit helps our spirit understand this, as He fills in the details, bringing the Truth of Scripture to mind.

THE PLAN UNFOLDING, A PROGRESSIVE REVELATION

The Truth is, it takes a Revelation from God Himself to see what He has in store for those who have accepted His Perfect Plan of Salvation, and where the Plan is going.

The purpose of God in revealing "The Plan" to men and angels was for "the Created" to see and know that His Will and Ways are best for "the Creation." As the Creator-Revealer, He chose beforehand to make His Will and the outcome of the Plan known to us.[3] As Eternal God, He has already seen the outcome of those who have chosen obedience, and those who have chosen rebellion, those who have rejected the Plan and Purposes of God. For our part, the Plan of God centers on the Promise, "The Promise" given to humanity after the fall. "To Eve, God gave the Promise of a Redeemer," One whose heel would crush the author of sin; for all who believe, He is the hope of man's salvation. We become Heirs of the Promise by believing and receiving what God has said. By faith, we know He will fulfill it; He has given His Word in Advance. When a person understands "the Big Picture," they go from a mind-set of independence and rebellion against God and His Plan, to one of dependence, trusting, believing in, and obeying His Word, and from there to one of interdependence. Our Salvation thrives in interdependence, as we come into His family. We love and worship Him and serve His children, our brothers, and sisters in Christ, knowing that whatever we have done to the least of them, we have done to Him. [4] This, too, is a part of His Purpose.

> *The LORD of Hosts has sworn, saying, Surely, as I have thought and planned, so shall it come to pass, and as I have purposed, so shall it stand—*[5]

God set the Master Plan up on the decrees and promises found in His Word. "The Big Picture" unfolds and comes into clearer view when we understand these decrees and promises. God gave us His Word for the Creation to watch and see it fulfilled. The purpose of the Plan is to end the sin of man (again sin means "falling short and missing the mark"). The sinful nature is the work of the devil, displayed in Creation and in the lives of those who belong to him. God's purpose is to stop the author of sin, the Devil. For it is written, "He who sins is of the devil, for the devil has sinned from the beginning. For this purpose, the Son of God was manifested, that He might destroy the works of the devil. Whoever has been born of God does not sin, for His seed is still in him; and he cannot sin, because he has been born of God. In this the children of God and the children of the devil are manifest: Whoever does not practice righteousness is not of God, nor *is* he who does not love his brother."[6]

He, "Who is, Who was and Who is to come," is fulfilling the Father's Will, and the decrees, promises and purposes found in His Plan. "Let's look at some of the Purposes found in the Masters Plan," they are:

To fulfill the Promise given to Eve, and to Abraham,

To fulfill the Law and the Prophets,

To expose the guilt of sin,

To provide the Perfect Sacrifice for Sin, doing away with disobedience, making atonement, and washing our sins away,

To allow Christ sacrifice to substitute for our sin, thus setting the captives free from the power and fear of death,

To reveal and explain the reality of the Kingdom,

To reveal and let men see what the Father is like,

To reveal and fulfill the Master's Plan,

To Save the Lost,

To reveal Christ as, 'the Type' of Person He wants His children to become,

To redeem the "whosoever wills" among man, bringing many sons and daughters to glory,

To create new spiritual offspring,

To give gifts to men for Gathering and Equipping His Church,

To give men the power to resist the enemy of their souls,

To destroy the works of the Devil,

To show His wisdom in all its rich variety to the rulers and authorities in the heavenly realms,

To set up an Eternal Kingdom on Earth and Restore Order to Creation.

As incredible as the Plan seems, we can see why God has a purpose in revealing it. Thus, it was our God Who said, "I make known the end from the beginning, from ancient times, what is still to come. I say: My Purpose will stand, and I will do all that I please. From the east I summon a bird of prey; from a far-off land, a man to fulfill My Purpose. *What I have Said, that Will I bring about; What I have Planned, that Will I Do.*"[7]

Knowing there is a Plan makes us willing to be part of it. Our goal is to spread God's Good News. The Holy Spirit convicts Unbelievers and convinces Believers of the truth about Jesus Christ. He does this through our witness and testimony. The Spirit anoints Believers to be Ambassadors and Representatives of God. For we must tell them that, "All this newness of life is from God, Who brought us back to Himself through what Christ did.

And God has given us the task of reconciling people to Him. For God was in Christ, reconciling the world to Himself, no longer counting people's sins against them. This is the wonderful message He has given us to tell others.

We are Christ's ambassadors, and God is using us to speak to you. We urge you, as though Christ Himself were here pleading with you, "Be reconciled to God!" For God made Christ, Who never sinned, to be the offering for our sin, so that we could be made right with God through Christ." [8] In the Great Commission Christ sent disciples forth to proclaim the Good News. He sent us to preach Salvation, not sociology; evangelism, not economics; redemption, not reform; transformation, not culture; pardon, not progress; new birth, not a new social order; regeneration, not revolution; revival, not renovation; resurrection, not reincarnation; a New Creation, not reorganization; faith in the Gospel, not democracy; *"Christ and not the traditions of men."*

Our goal is to share with others the mystery of His unfolding Plan. Our intent is "to explain to everyone this Plan that God, the Creator of all things, had kept secret from the beginning,"[9] "This is the Plan of God, Who *Created All Things* through Jesus Christ." (See Ephesians Chapter 3). See other references to this Mystery in 1Corinthians 2:7; 4:1; Ephesians 3:4, 9; 5:32; 6:19; Colossians 2:2; 4:3; 1Timothy 3:9, 16.

DIVINE PURPOSES

All the Divine Purposes follow His Plan. God does not waste anything; He had His Purpose in mind, even before one-third of the angels fell, following Satan in pride, sin, rebellion, and ruin. The Word says, "He didn't create the earth void or empty, He created it for habitation."[10] As we will see, Divine Judgment made the earth void and empty. For in Genesis 1:2 we read, "Now the earth was {Or possibly became} formless and empty, darkness was over the surface of the deep, and the Spirit of God was hovering over the waters." Nevertheless, even before God created man on the earth, or before He came to restore it to an inhabitable state during the 6 days of earth's restoration (Genesis 1:3-2:4). God had a Plan.

The LORD works out everything for His own ends—even the wicked for a day of disaster.[11]

The Divine Purposes are Irresistible. Life has so much more meaning when we live knowing the Father's in control. Nothing can thwart His purposes, "His Kingdom will come, and His Will be done on Earth, as it is in Heaven." [12] When we know that whatever He allows now, He allows for a greater good than we, from our earthly perspective, can fully realize, or understand. For while He didn't say "everything," He did say, "All things" work together for good to them that love God, to them who are called according to His purpose."[13] He is effecting changes in both the spiritual and the physical realms, as He works out His Plan of restoration and order in Creation. For now, the focus of the Plan is on the Church and bringing the last members into the Body of Christ.[14] The LORD Almighty has spoken—who can change His Plans? When His hand moves, who can stop Him?"[15] Who has resisted His Will?

The Divine Purposes are sure of Fulfillment. God's Word gives us foreknowledge of His purposes; for example, "Babylon trembles and writhes in pain, for everything the LORD has planned against her stands unchanged. Babylon will be left desolate without a single inhabitant."[16] While this prophecy has so far had only partial fulfillment, it stands like so many that will one day be complete. Modern day Iraq now stands on the land once called the Babylon empire; and even now, the great city of Babylon is secretly being rebuilt. With all the effort to make Iraq a democratic nation now, there are certain events that will take place in Iraq's future, which, when aligned, will qualify it for God's judgment and bring fulfillment to this prophecy. (See Revelation Chapter 18).

> "WITH ALL THE EFFORT TO MAKE IRAQ A DEMOCRATIC NATION NOW, THERE ARE CERTAIN EVENTS THAT WILL TAKE PLACE IN IRAQ'S FUTURE, WHICH WHEN ALIGNED, WILL QUALIFY IT FOR GOD'S JUDGMENT AND BRING FULFILLMENT TO THIS PROPHECY."

God honors His Word above His name. The Bible states and the LORD declared, "Heaven and Earth will pass away, but My Word will never pass away."[17]

This present Earth and its surrounding heaven will pass away, and God will create a "New Heavens and a new Earth." This is right out of His Word.[18]

If there is anything that we can count on, it is this, what God has said and purposed He will fulfill. "Our God is the God Who calls those things that are not as though they were;" He speaks of the nonexistent, which He has foretold and promised as if it existed; He speaks of future events with as much certainty as if, they had already come to pass.[19] "God keeps His Word."

The Divine Purposes are revealed in His choice of Instruments. God displays His Power in those chosen to fulfill various parts of the Plan. This is where men through obedience find Purpose, with the Word and Spirit of God working in, and through, them. We see examples of God's chosen instruments throughout the Plan, "those who stood in the gap," in both Old and New Testaments. The LORD exalts one and the LORD brings another one low. God raised up Pharaoh, who persecuted Israel when He called the Nation out of Egypt.[20] The Word says, "But I have raised you up for this very Purpose, that I might show you My Power and that My Name might be proclaimed in all the earth."[21] Who among us has not heard of God's deliverance of Israel out of Egypt? God's power is revealed and displayed in those chosen throughout His-story as instruments to carry out His Purposes and do His will. The Word says, "It is not by might, nor by power, but by My Spirit, thus says the LORD."[22]

CHRIST IS THE POWER AND THE WISDOM OF GOD

As Believers we stand with the Apostle Paul, "For the message of the cross is foolishness to those who are perishing, but to us who are being saved it is the Power of God.

For it is written:

"I will destroy the wisdom of the wise and bring to nothing the understanding of the prudent." Where *is* the wise? Where *is* the scribe? Where *is* the disputer of this Age? Has not God made foolish the wisdom of this world? For since, in the wisdom of God, the world through wisdom did not know God, it pleased God through the foolishness of the message preached to save those who believe.

For Jews request a sign, and Greeks {Gentiles} look for wisdom; but we preach Christ crucified, to the Jews a stumbling block and to the Greeks foolishness, but to those who are called, both Jews and Greeks, Christ the power of God and the wisdom of God. Because the foolishness of God is wiser than men, and the weakness of God is stronger than men.

For you see your calling, brethren, that not many wise according to the flesh, not many mighty, not many noble, *are called.* But God has chosen the foolish things of the world to put to shame the wise, and God has chosen the weak things of the world to put to shame the things which are mighty; and the base things of the world and the things which are despised God has chosen, and the things which are not, to bring to nothing the things that are, that no flesh should glory in His presence.

But of Him you are in Christ Jesus, who became for us wisdom from God—and righteousness and sanctification and redemption—that, as it is written, *"He who glories, let him glory in the LORD."*[23]

By the Spirit, God Fulfills His purposes.
He works in those willing to do His Will.

The Divine Purposes are revealed in the Gospels. We see God's Plan in the face of His Son. It was the work of Christ that wrought our deliverance, restoring the fellowship broken by sin. God prearranged everything needed to restore man into fellowship with Himself, through the work of His Son.

The Gospels reveal many of God's purposes, but they all have one thing in common, they all focus on the birth, life, ministry, death, and resurrection of the Lord Jesus Christ. The Father sent Him to fulfill His Word; in Christ, the Father thrust the Divine Purpose to the forefront, when He raised Him from the Dead. [24]

Our purpose is to share the "Good News" at the center of God's Plan and Purpose. For its not the Father's desire that any should perish, but that all should hear and receive the "Good News" and come to repentance.[25] The Father has delighted to make everything known to us "in Christ", "And He made known to us the Mystery of His Will according to His good pleasure, which He purposed in Christ."[26] "The Good News" is only the beginning of new life. We will arise, just as He did, not to our old way of life and nature (living and thinking), but to new life, and the new nature, through the transforming power which God made available for us in Him (Christ). Our challenge is to grow daily in the wisdom and knowledge of God, seeking to know His suffering, His victory, and the power of His resurrection.[27] His example affects His purposes for our lives, in every way, as He leads us in the here and now through the anointing work and power of the Holy Spirit and a growing knowledge of His Word. Thus, God gives us the means to walk in new life, new power, and new light (Truth). Once we realize that God has provided everything for our growing in grace and knowledge of Him, the victories, which you and I grasp, come about as we walk, led by the Holy Spirit, in our new life in Christ.[28]

"Truth is, while the water of life flows in full view of all,
only the thirsty dare drink of it."

Lastly, the Divine Purpose involves the overthrow of Satan and restoring order to Creation. Now, "He who does what is sinful is of the devil because the devil has been sinning from the beginning. The reason that the Son of God appeared was to destroy the devil's work."[29]

During His Ministry on earth, Jesus taught and gave many parables to the people; He used this mystery style of teaching to explain many truths about the kingdom. These mysteries held hidden truths about the kingdom, but only those who wanted to understand chose to ask and sought to know there hidden meaning.

On one occasion, Jesus said, "Listen to another parable:

There was a landowner who planted a vineyard. He put a wall around it, dug a winepress in it, and built a watchtower. Then He rented the vineyard to some farmers and went away on a journey. When the time of harvest approached, He sent His servants to the tenants to collect His fruit. "The tenants seized His servants; they beat one, killed another, and stoned a third. Then He sent other servants to them, more than the first time, and the tenants treated them in the same way.

"Last of all, He sent His Son to them. 'They will respect My Son,' He said. But when the tenants saw the Son, they said to each other, 'This is the Heir." Come, let us kill him and take His inheritance.' So, they took Him and threw Him out of the vineyard and killed Him." [30]

The Landowner Who planted the vineyard is the Father. The farmers are Satan and the spiritual rulers of darkness; the tenants were the *leaders* of Israel, some of whom were children of the Devil. The Servants whom they seized, and either beat, killed or stoned, were the Prophets and Messengers sent throughout the Age to warn the people, and turn them back to God. Finally, the Father (the Landowner) sent His Son saying, *'They will respect My Son.'* Now, what the spiritual rulers of this Age did was to refuse to offer the Creator the fruits of His earth, committed to their care. They rejected His merciful pleadings, and, in the end, they destroyed whatever hopes might have still been to them by crying: *This is the Heir! Come, let us kill Him, that the inheritance may be ours!"* Now, just as believers follow the lead of their Father. The Bible makes it clear from the account given of Judas (the one who betrayed Him) that these earthly rulers were simply following the lead of their father and

> "THIS IS THE HEIR! COME, LET US KILL HIM, THAT THE INHERITANCE MAY BE OURS!"

the rulers of darkness over men. Jesus had already said to them, "You are of your father, the devil, and it is your will to practice the lusts and gratify the desires *which are characteristic* of your father. He was a murderer from the beginning, and does not stand in the truth, because there is no truth in him. When he speaks a falsehood, he speaks what is natural to him, for he is a liar *himself* and the father of lies and of all that is false.[31] Thus, these men were simply following those spiritual forces who prompted them to crucify the Lord of Glory. These are the rulers of the darkness of this Age of whom, the Apostle Paul was referring when He spoke of the saints putting on the whole armor of God. (See Ephesians 6:12).

These agencies never suspected God's foreknowledge, or the "secret wisdom," concerning Christ resurrection and victory over death. Paul later said, "We do, however, speak a message of wisdom among the mature, but not the wisdom of this *Age* or of the rulers of this *Age*, who are coming to nothing. No, we speak of God's secret wisdom, a wisdom that has been hidden and that *God destined for our glory before time began. None of the Rulers of this Age understood it*, for if they had, they would not have crucified the LORD of Glory."[32]

Again, sin, iniquity, transgression and disobedience made it necessary for a Savior, Deliverer and Mediator. God has given man this gift, in the person of His Son.

Part 4 –

Light From the
Prophetic Word

CHAPTER 9

Prophecy: The Plan Given

By Faith, the Old Testament Saints looked forward to the First Coming. By Faith, the New Testament Saints look forward to the Second. By Faith, we looked forward.

THE SPIRIT OF PROPHECY

The Word and Work of Jesus Christ are "the foundation" and "the cornerstone" of God's unchanging Plan. He is the Head, and the Church is His body.[1] His body consists of people of Faith and Prophecy. The Word is our Source of Faith. Through His Word and Work, we have the knowledge of Prophecy. God's Word is about carrying all His Plans and Purposes for this present Creation forward, and has everything to do with fulfilling the Prophecies and Promises found in It. Never forget, *"God is all about His Word, He keeps it."*

Together, the written prophecies reveal the past and future works of God in His Creation. This is why it is so important to hear what He has said. God inspired the Prophets to Prophesy; He inspired men to write the Bible. Listen; you and I both know the world is getting darker; the Word prophesied that this would happen a long time ago, before the glorious day dawns. We are on the verge of a new day, a day when the Morning Star, "the Daystar," will arise. For our Salvation is much closer than when we first believed. Because of what we can now see, we have even greater confidence in the message proclaimed by the prophets. The Spirit warning us to, "Pay close attention to what they wrote, for their words are like a light shining in a dark place—until the day Christ appears and His brilliant light shines in your hearts. Above all, you must understand that no prophecy in Scripture ever came from the prophets themselves or because they wanted to prophesy. It was the Holy Spirit Who moved the prophets to speak from God."[2]

Looking down through the corridors of time, God moved on men pre-chosen for the task of writing and preserving what He chose to reveal to man. Prophecy came as the Spirit of God moved on men who spoke and wrote portions of the Master's Plan. The Spirit, searching the mind of God—inspired men to write; they wrote as God moved them.

The rain and snow come down from the heavens and stay on the ground to water the earth. They cause the grain to grow, producing seed for the farmer and bread for the hungry. It is the same with My Word. I send It out, and It always produces fruit. It will carry out all I want It to, and It will prosper everywhere I send It.[3]

Individual Prophecies in the Word are like pieces of a puzzle, parts of the whole. "In many separate revelations each of which set forth a portion of the Truth and in different ways God spoke of old to our forefathers in and by the Prophets." [4] God gave Prophecy in a piecemeal fashion, a part here, a part there, here a little, there a little, line upon line, precept upon precept. Like someone reading a book at various times, at various places over hundreds of years, the Spirit searching the mind of God chose and inspired men to write the Prophetic Word. They wrote in different countries, men from various backgrounds and occupations spoke and wrote the Thoughts and Words of God. Every prophetic word uttered, had some bearing on the immediate or future work of God. Again, all prophecy has its roots in the foreknowledge of God, revealing Himself through the Spirit of Prophecy.[5] The Holy Spirit spoke through men to reveal God's Plan and arrangements for our Salvation. While the 66 books of the Bible hold the parts of the Plan, it is those portions on Prophecy, roughly one third of the Bible, which show us where the Plan is going.

> "AGAIN, ALL PROPHECY HAS ITS ROOTS IN THE FOREKNOWLEDGE OF GOD, REVEALING HIMSELF THROUGH THE SPIRIT OF PROPHECY."

PROPHECY: KEY TO UNDERSTANDING THE PLAN

The study of Prophecy is the study of His-Story written in advance. God used the prophets to give man a progressive revelation of Himself. Thus, through prophecy, we find the key to understanding the Plan, as Jesus taught many of the messages contained in the Law, the Prophets, and the Psalms clearly unfolded and found fulfillment in the New Testament.

The revelations found in the prophetic writings—from Moses to Malachi, from the Garden of Eden to the call of the forerunner, "John the Baptist"—all work to reveal and find perfect fulfillment in one Man, "the Lord Jesus Christ." He is the great subject of Prophecy. He said, "These are the Words which I spoke to you while I was still with you, that all things must be fulfilled which were written in the Law of Moses, and the Prophets and the Psalms concerning Me."[6] At His first coming, Jesus fulfilled many of the Old Testament Prophecies; however, He left many of them unfulfilled, He even added some new ones before He went back to heaven, which meant, "He's Coming Again." *He spoke of His coming again.*[7]

Prophecy reveals the Word and Work of God. The Messages preserved in the Prophetic writings reveal what God wanted us to know. Some prophecies were unconditional with God telling man in advance what would happen in the future. Others were conditional, holding a promise of blessing for obedience, or warnings of judgment for disobedience. Some prophecies warned those who refused to repent and continue down a certain path, but if they turned, they would avoid His wrath. We find one such example of this in the third Chapter of the book of Jonah, and the account of the city of Nineveh. (See Jonah 3:1-10). While blessings were sure for obedience, warnings of judgment held periods of grace, short or long. What the Father wants from man is trust and obedience, for us to walk with Him, and when we fail, repentance, turning from sin, and getting back on course, back into a right relationship with Him. This is a common theme throughout the Holy record. For although God has kept many things hidden, the prophetic record holds everything He wanted us to know about His Plan, those things, which would eventually come to pass.

A PLANNED REVELATION

But what is Prophecy? Prophecy is the foretelling of future events. Prophecy like Foreknowledge is the knowledge of events before they happen. For even though Prophecy extends over thousands of years, without prophecy there would be no knowledge of the Plan. The distinction between foreknowledge and prophecy is that prophecy is a revelation of that foreknowledge, those portions of foreknowledge that God chose to make known to man. True prophecy never began with man, for prophecy never came by the will of man. Therefore, "If it's not from God, it's false and meant to deceive."

Scriptural prophecy and prophetic revelations are gifts of Christ. The Father gave revelations through Christ, and the Holy Spirit to representatives chosen in advance. The Prophetic Word is a Divine Message.

The Message: Word Given, Word Fulfilled

In the many Messages, God reveals His Plan and Purposes for the Salvation of man. Not only is God, "the Author of Creation," [8] "the Author of Life" [9] and "the Author of our Salvation." [10] He is also, "the Author and Finisher of our FAITH," [11] and "the Author of all True Prophecy," this includes prophetic visions and dreams. The Father is the source of the Message, God sent "The Message, He sent His Word," Jesus is the Word. It is our intent in this work to show just how the Son fulfilled the Message. He gave the clear purpose of the Message. He told them saying, "Do not think that I have come to do away with or undo the Law or the Prophets; I have come not to do away with or undo but to complete and fulfill them." [12] From the beginning, it was the Holy Spirit Who inspired men to write the Message. Jesus said, "For truly I tell you, until the sky and earth pass away and perish, not one smallest letter nor one little hook (*identifying certain Hebrew letters*) will pass from the Law until all things *it foreshadows* are accomplished." [13]

Listen, God's Will, Plan and Purpose will find fulfillment. From the beginning, God gave prophecies to and through those chosen to be His representatives. God used them to sculpt for us, an image of the person and work of the One Who would come. Therefore, having so many witnesses who saw Him fulfill these prophecies, and leaving us a written account, we identify Him as "the Christ." Even from the lips of doubting Thomas, came the words, "My Lord and my God." [14]

THE PROPHETS

Gods Plan is one of, "tell and show, He tells us then He shows us." For, "Surely the Sovereign LORD does nothing without revealing His Plan to His servants the PROPHETS. The lion has roared—who will not fear? The Sovereign LORD has spoken—who can but PROPHESY?" [15]

Gods hand and calling was on all the true Prophets. Both, the Prophets, and Christ gave us Revelations from God. God raised them up, appointed and sent them. He filled them with and moved them by the Holy Spirit. They spoke with authority, in the name of the LORD. As God's representatives, the people esteemed them as "Holy Men": Seers; Men of God; Prophets of God; Holy prophets and Holy men of God. God gave spokeswomen to share the Message also. The Prophets were the Messengers and Servants of God, the Watchmen of Israel. The Prophets spoke in the name of the LORD; they often spoke in parables and riddles or in their actions made signs to the people. However, many times, there was a dearth, with no Divine communication because of the sins of the people. To Israel, God said, "I spoke to the Prophets, gave them many Visions and told Parables through them."[16] The LORD used a Prophet to bring Israel up from Egypt, by a Prophet He cared for him.[17]

God has been speaking through men to man for a longtime.

The Old and New Testament Messengers

In the Old Testament, they were the Seers and Prophets in the New, Prophets, Apostles, and members of the body of Christ. The person, who spoke for God, spoke with the voice of a Prophet. The Prophets were conduits, spokespersons, and representatives of the living God. God spoke and wrote through these chosen vessels. The Messages flowed from the Spiritual into this physical realm.

As instruments of the Spirit of God, they carried Messages from heaven, from the throne, directly from the mouth of God. They spoke the Word of God, many beginning with "Thus says the LORD."

The Old Testament Prophets consisted of two groups called "the Major, and the Minor Prophets." Not only did they speak, but they also wrote, thus preserving the Messages for us. It was the *extent of their writings*, which made them either "Major or Minor Prophets." The Major Prophets lived from about 740 to 540 B.C. These were Isaiah, Jeremiah, Ezekiel, and Daniel. The Minor Prophets lived from about 800 to 400 B.C. These were Hosea, Joel, Amos, Obadiah, Jonah, Micah, Nahum, Habakkuk, Zephaniah, Haggai, Zechariah, and Malachi.

While some of their prophecies had immediate fulfillment, many pointed to some future time or event, and not fulfilled during the lifetime of the Prophet. Again, God gave the Plan, here a line, there a part, with keys about the future contained in what they prophesied, which when connected and placed in order, spoke of the work of Christ. Some spoke of His first coming, others His Second, while the rest had to do with events surrounding his return. It was the Spirit of God, which caused men to speak, act, and do what the Father wanted done: through inspiration, they spoke and wrote the Words that God gave them.

WHAT ARE THE ODDS OF A PROPHETIC FULFILLMENT?

Let us turn for a moment and look at the chance and odds of a prophetic fulfillment. If someone were to predict that a certain volcano would erupt next year, the chance of this occurring would be 1 in 2. If they were to add another prediction that it would happen on August 28, chances now decrease to 1 in 4. Add another detail and it becomes 1 in 8, so on and so forth, up to 11 details, then, the chance of it happening goes to 1 in 2,048.

Looking at the Scriptures, we see not one, not two, but over a 100 prophecies fulfilled by one man during a short lifetime of 33 years, with more than 25 of them fulfilled in a 24-hour period. Taking the odds of our example, the chances of one man fulfilling just the 25 predictions would be 1 in 33,554,432. Now, when you consider that Moses and the prophets who wrote them lived anywhere from 1,500 to 400 years before the birth of Christ, you get some idea of the scope of God's Plan. Christ fulfilled over 100 prophecies during His First Coming. The odds of this being accidental are one in trillions. Think of what this means. If you have any prophetic knowledge, stop, and consider those prophecies, to be fulfilled at His "Second Coming."

"CHRIST FULFILLED OVER 100 PROPHECIES DURING HIS FIRST COMING. THE ODDS OF THIS BEING ACCIDENTAL ARE ONE IN TRILLIONS."

The Word is "Sure," [18] in other words, "if God said it, you could take it to the bank; He's going to fulfill it." The record of accomplishment of fulfilled prophecy is 100 percent to the letter, thus making unfulfilled prophecy 100 percent sure of fulfillment. Unfulfilled Prophecy provides an outline of the future, and because of this, "Biblical Prophecy is not some guess at a future event, Prophecy is the *'Event,'* as it will unfold, revealed beforehand."

Prophetic Types and Test

Whether spoken or written, some prophecies had immediate fulfillment, while others pointed to some future event. Many never saw fulfillment during the lifetime of the Prophet, thus providing those who were alive during its fulfillment, proof the prophet had indeed been a Messenger sent from God. To qualify as legitimate Prophecy, the event spoken of had to be beyond all human foresight and knowledge; give specific details and have enough time-lapses between the prediction and its fulfillment; thus, preventing the predictor from fulfilling it. At some point, there had to be clear and obvious proof of its fulfillment. Some prophecies reveal the law of double reference meaning, "more than one fulfillment in space and time," having a partial fulfillment in the past, with a greater fulfillment at some yet, future date. (Compare Joel 2:28-32 and Acts 2:16-21). Then, there is another "Type" of Prophecy, which transcends time. A type in which the prophet begins to speak of a matter of their day, is then suddenly, borne by the Spirit, to some breathtaking event. The Prophet so caught up, as if he were a time

> NOW WHAT MAKES THE SCRIPTURES SO UNIQUE IS THAT IT CONTAINS HUNDREDS OF PROPHECIES.

traveler, transported in the Spirit through space and time. He spoke of past, present, or future events, which before that time had still been veiled, the event of his own day, a faint "type or shadow" of the far greater one. Now what makes the Scriptures so unique is that It holds hundreds of Prophecies. Events which the Almighty foresaw and inspired men to write or speak, often hundreds of years before they happened. Taking them together the prophecies reveal the past, seen in prophecies fulfilled (history), the present, and the future, these being either prophetic events that are seeing fulfillment now, or aligning themselves for future fulfillment. The foreknowledge of God gave all of this to us in advance. For Believers, life is both interesting and exciting when we realize that right now, both men and angels are eagerly waiting to see Gods Word and Works unfold in Creation.

Here are some of the Major Prophecies in the Word:

(See chart at the end of this chapter).

The *Times of the Gentiles* began with king Nebuchadnezzar[19] (606 B.C.), which will end at the *Second Coming of Christ. The Birth of Christ, the First Coming.*[20] (5-4 B.C.). *The Sacrifice of God's Lamb* on the Cross followed by, *"The Resurrection."*[21] (30 A.D.).

Pentecost, the Church begun, with God giving us the Holy Spirit.[22] (From 30 A.D. until the present, almost 2000 yrs.). *The fall and destruction of Jerusalem.*[23] (70 A.D.). *The Return of the Jews,* to form the Nation of Israel (1948 A.D.).

The Rapture, the (secret) coming of Christ, as a thief in the night, *"for His Church,"* to take Believers to heaven.[24] *The (Bema) Judgment Seat of Christ* where Christ judges Believers, rewarding them for their faithful service, while they were on earth.[25] *The Great Apostasy*, the falling away from the Faith;[26] *The Great Tribulation;*[27] the earth undergoing seven years of distress, also known as the time of *"Jacob's Trouble."*[28] The rise and eventual fall of, *"the False Prophet and Antichrist."*[29] God's Judgment of *Religious and Commercial Babylon,*[30] followed by *the Battle of Armageddon* with *the Antichrist and False Prophet cast alive into "the Lake of fire."*[31]

The (visible) *Second Coming of Christ, "with His Church,"* to judge and rule over the Nations of the earth.[32] Christ separating the sheep from the goat nations.[33] This will mark the beginning of the next Age on the earth, with Satan bound for 1000 yrs.[34] *The Millennial* (1000 yr.) *Kingdom* begins, with the Saints ruling with Christ and *Israel Head of the Nations.*[35] Following the Millennial Kingdom, we see *the Last Great Rebellion of Satan* (Satan's Last Revolt).[36]

The Earth renovated by Fire[37] (purged of sin), during the time of *the Great White Throne Judgment,*[38] this is the last resurrection with all the unsaved judged, and finally, God revealing *the New Heavens and New Earth.*[39] After putting an end to all rule and all authority and power, we will then see the Son delivering everything up to the Father that God may be "all in all." (See 1Corinthians 15:24-28). This will complete God's restoration of order to His Kingdom, this old becoming a new creation, made up of faithful angels and the redeemed. Indeed, all this must happen. The Major Prophecies laid out in brief order above reveal where the Plan is going. It is important that Saints see this if they want to develop an eternal mind-set, and begin living to fulfill their calling, realizing what we do now will influence our reward and place in eternity ahead of us. For us, the next major event on the prophetic calendar is *"the Rapture,"* which can happen at any moment. This is why an affirmative response to the Message of Hope is so urgent.

The Word Reveals the Past, Present, and the Future

Because the Word reveals the past, with confidence we can look back at the Prophetic record of accomplishment, see the prophecies already fulfilled, and know that we have the Truth; all of this serves to confirm and strengthen our Faith. On the other hand, the Word of God says that "the god of this world" has blinded the minds of them who do not believe.[40] Now, "if the blind lead the blind, shall they not both fall into a ditch?" Having rejected the "Author of the Plan," men walk, groping in darkness, trying to feel their way into an uncertain future.

"Because they have rejected the Truth, they have no firm foundation for either understanding the past or seeing the future."

We can see the Word revealing the present when we know which prophecies have happened, and which ones have not. We have some idea of where we stand in the prophetic timetable. By placing unfulfilled prophecies in an intelligent and most likely order of fulfillment, looking at the present and the various Scriptures, which show the last day's signs, we can see that we are close to the Rapture. Thus, like a marker in space and time, prophetic alignment confirms the faith of believers in the present. While revealing we are close, it is obvious "the Rapture" has not happened yet.

The Word reveals the future. Again, by looking at unfulfilled prophecy and events taking place in the world around us, with optimism we can see events aligning themselves and setting the stage for future fulfillment.

Unfulfilled, prophesied conditions are like lights, signs showing the future. For example, the continuing *deception* of the masses by mass media, the *rise of evil men* and women, and would be (false) Christ, *wars and rumors of wars*.[41] Look around you, *terrorism, financial upheavals, changing weather patterns, natural disasters, famine, genocide, mass poverty, and earthquakes*, the increase in intensity and frequency, provide us with many clues. We watch as the Creation labors and groans in the sorrows of "birth pangs," to give birth to a new creation. Those holding a temporal, Liberal, Socio-internationalist (Globalist, one-worlder's) worldview, purposefully encourage the widening rift between believers and nonbelievers, who in promoting a temporal one world agenda see Christianity as an obstacle standing in their way and opposing their progress. Political correctness and other doctrines of demons (whom many do not believe exist) are exposing themselves as an effective tool in the rise and growth of this secular humanist agenda. Expressions like "Global this or that," Tolerance, Multiculturalism, Hate Speech, these are just a few words in the Liberal lexicon of new-speak. While they themselves are anti-Tolerant, anti-God, anti-Nation, anti-Cultural, and anti-Love, when it comes to the Christian Faith. Sadly, the names of those *not* written in the Lamb's book of life stand caught in the sway and snare of the enemy, caught in a delusion, and committed to spreading, "the Lie."[42]

All of this confirms the truth of the conflict between those in the light and those still in darkness. The subtle and obvious parts of this conflict are visible in all arenas of life. They display their hatred by their increased hostility and not so subtle attacks on the Christian Faith, like their spiritual ancestors, they oppose the Rule of Christ. They hate Him, even though most of them do not know why; they reveal themselves to be puppets of an unseen enemy. Combined, world events are aligning as forerunners, "signs" setting the stage for the imminent "Rapture of the Saints" which again we believe to be the next major event in the Prophetic calendar.

Through Prophecy, He has given us the Big Picture of His Plan.

As you look to understand the Prophetic Word, focus on Him, for He reminds us saying, "You search and investigate and pour over the Scriptures diligently, because you suppose and trust that you have eternal life through them. And these *very Scriptures* testify about Me![43] He also said, "But when the Father sends the Counselor as My representative —and by the Counselor I mean the Holy Spirit —He will teach you everything and will remind you of everything I myself have told you.[44] He will guide you into all truth; for He will not speak on His own authority, but whatever He hears He will speak; and He will tell you *things to come.*[45]

THE PURPOSE OF PROPHECY

Prophecy understood does much to defeat "a vain sense of hope," providing reassurance that our Hope of Salvation stands on a solid foundation, satisfying our wish to know, it helps us prepare for our future. The Prophets knew there was a Cross and a Crown. "They searched attentively and with the greatest care, trying to find out the time and circumstances to which the Spirit of Christ in them was pointing when He Predicted the Sufferings of Christ and the Glories that would follow."

The New Living Translation states it this way:

This salvation was something the prophets wanted to know more about. They prophesied about this gracious salvation prepared for you, even though they had many questions as to what it all could mean. They wondered what the Spirit of Christ within them was talking about when He told them in advance about Christ's suffering and His great glory afterward.

They wondered when and to whom all this would happen. They were told that these things would not happen during their lifetime, but many years later, during yours. And now this Good News has been announced by those who preached to you in the power of the Holy Spirit sent from heaven. It is all so wonderful that even the angels are eagerly watching these things happen. So think clearly and exercise self-control. Look forward to the special blessings that will come to you at the return of Jesus Christ.[46]

While "The Message" says the same passage this way:

> *The prophets who told us this was coming asked a lot of questions about this gift of life God was preparing. The Messiah's Spirit let them in on some of it—that the Messiah would experience suffering, followed by glory. They clamored to know who and when. All they were told was that they were serving you, you who by orders from heaven have now heard for yourselves—through the Holy Spirit—the Message of those prophecies fulfilled. Do you realize how fortunate you are? Angels would have given anything to be in on this! So roll up your sleeves, put your mind in gear, be totally ready to receive the gift that's coming when Jesus arrives.47*

"Rejoice, for It has been given to you to know the mysteries of the Kingdom of Heaven."

Listen it is all real and God did it all for us. Just think, you are part of the Mystery of mysteries. When the seventy that He sent out to share the Message returned with joy and news of the results, some of them rejoiced saying Lord, even the demons are subject to us in Your name. "Yes," He told them, "I saw Satan falling from heaven as a flash of lightning! (See Luke 10:18). And I have given you authority over all the power of the enemy, and you can walk among snakes and scorpions and crush them. Nothing will injure you. But do not rejoice just because evil spirits obey you; rejoice because your names are registered as citizens of heaven." Then Jesus was filled with the joy of the Holy Spirit and said, "O Father, Lord of heaven and earth, thank you for hiding the truth from those who think themselves so wise and clever, and for revealing it to the childlike. Yes, Father, it pleased you to do it this way. My Father has given Me authority over everything. No one really knows the Son except the Father, and no one really knows the Father except the Son and those to whom the Son chooses to reveal Him." Then when they were alone, He turned to the disciples and said, "How privileged you are to see what you have seen. I tell you, many prophets and kings have longed to see and hear what you have seen and heard, but they could not."[48] This was God's purpose in giving us the prophetic Word. All of this, Christ did for our Salvation. The disciples were living witnesses, as

God was fulfilling His Word. God has given that same Word to us, "For everything that was written in the past was written to teach us, so that through endurance and the encouragement of the Scriptures we might have Hope."[49] As Believers, our hope increases as we give heed to the prophecies, receiving them by FAITH.

In many places throughout the Word, God declares a blessing on those who read, hear, trust, and obey His Word. Paul said, "God can make you strong, just as the Good News says. It is the Message about Jesus Christ and His Plan for you Gentiles, a Plan kept Secret from the Beginning of time. But now as the Prophets foretold and as the Eternal God has commanded, this Message is made known to all Gentiles everywhere, so that they might believe and obey Christ."[50] (See Ephesians 3:1-11).

This is the purpose of Prophecy; this is the way that God chose to let us know.

On the Authority of the vibrant, Living Word of God, we have the keys by which we can know everything God wanted man to know. It is our source of confident hope as the Living God works out His Plan and Purposes in Creation. If God said it, it is going to happen, you can take it to the Bank; there is nothing that men or angels can do to stop it.

Event	Paul	John	Peter	Christ	Malachi	Zechariah	Haggai	Obadiah	Ezekiel	Daniel	Jeremiah	Habakkuk	Zephaniah	Nahum	Isaiah	Micah	Amos	Hosea	Joel	Jonah	Enoch	Moses
The Times of the Gentiles										X	X											
The Birth of Christ											X				X	X						X
The Cross						X					X				X							
The Coming of the Holy Spirit							X												X			
The Destruction of Jerusalem										X												
The Church	X	X	X	X																		
The Return of the Jews									X		X				X	X		X				X
The Rapture	X																					
The Antichrist	X	X	X			X			X	X					X							
The Great Tribulation	X	X	X							X					X					X		
Armageddon		X				X			X				X		X					X		
The Second Coming	X	X		X		X			X													X
Judgment of the Nations			X	X																		
The Millennial Kingdom Begins	X	X				X			X	X			X	X	X	X	X	X		X		
Israel Head of the Nations									X	X					X							
Satan's Last Revolt		X																				
The Earth Renovated by Fire		X	X																			
The New Heavens and New Earth		X																X				

CHAPTER 10

The Plan Unveiled

The Spirit of Prophecy has given us "His Plan" in the Old and New Testaments.

As we said in the chapter on "Foreknowledge," God gave the big picture of His Plan through prophecy, which is His-Story, written in advance. When you see "the Big Picture," the mystery of the Plan begins to unfold. To unveil and present His Plan, God used "Revelation, Inspiration, and Illumination." God gradually revealed Himself, His Will, Plan and Purposes, through "Revelation," which we find hidden in the spoken and written Words of the Prophets. By "Inspiration," the Holy Spirit caused men to write the Scriptures. Under His power men spoke, wrote, and acted on what He revealed, being moved by what He was doing. For us "Illumination" or "Enlightenment" come when we, with God's help, rightly divide the Word, the Holy Spirit connecting the truth to our understanding. Thus, we realize that God did not give the Prophetic Word for our own private interpretation, but God has given us spiritual eyes to see spiritual truth. Only then can we see It as the Light of God, given to light the dark places of our understanding.

THE UNVEILING OF THE PLAN

By *Revelation*, God has given us the opportunity to increase our knowledge of Him and get a clearer picture of His Plan. By embracing the "Message of Truth," we take the first step in our exposure to the Plan. The Apostle Paul wrote, "But even if our Gospel (the glad tidings) also be hidden (obscured and covered up with a veil that hinders the knowledge of God), it is hidden *only* to those who are perishing and obscured *only* to those who are spiritually dying and veiled *only* to those who are lost. For the god of this world has blinded the unbelievers' minds *that they should not discern the truth*, preventing them from seeing the illuminating light of the Gospel of the Glory of Christ (the Messiah), Who is the Image and Likeness of God."[1] *My people are destroyed for lack of knowledge.*2

Through a new knowledge of God, God's people gain a changed worldview, a new perspective. The change does not take place in the Word of God; the change takes place within us. Our knowledge of the things of this life and temporal Age came through temporal eyes, a temporal mind-set conditioned by the rule of Satan, over the world and the flesh. "*Spiritual eyes open*, we now realize the plan of the enemy is that all humanity seeks their pleasure in and fix all our heartfelt hopes on this present Age over which he presides, as the god of this Age. That men use their best endeavors—by various sensuous and intellectual occupations and delights, and countless ways of killing time, which he has provided—to keep their thoughts from ever wandering over into that, "Age to come." That Age will find him a fettered captive, instead of a prince and a god.

This new knowledge comes to those who are new creations, having new eyes and a new understanding and a new or renewed faith in God and our Lord Jesus Christ. This happens when we realize that God wants to give us an eternal view of life. We also note here the Bible is God's revelation of Himself to man and that revelation is complete. God is not giving any new revelations; He is not adding any new books to the Bible. Our need is not for more books, or more revelations; our need is to understand what He has already given, for in fact, "Everything God wanted man to know; His Will, His Ways, and Plan, He sealed in His Word." There is no need for new Inspiration either; instead, what we need is Illumination, *the Holy Spirit opening our spiritual eyes and understanding, to what God has already revealed.* The Father gives knowledge of the Plan to those whom He draws to His Son. The Father gives those bound for Salvation to His Son. Jesus said, "Everything that the Father has is Mine." That is what I meant when I said that He *the Spirit* will take the things that are Mine and will reveal (declare, show, pass on) it to you.[3]

> *As Believers, we have access to the "Mind of Christ,"*[4] *the Mind of God. God wants you to have knowledge of His Plan.*

Now Inspiration was that special influence of the Holy Spirit, which led the Prophets and Biblical writers to speak and write what God wanted communicated. He did this without suspending their individuality or personality. The God of Truth inspired men to write the Holy Scriptures, the resulting "inspiration" making it reliable and dependable. It is the Authority of Scripture, rather than Its inspiration, which bear the weight of Scriptural writings about Its own nature. Passages such as "it is written," "It says" and "the Scripture says" clearly imply the total authority of the Scriptures. Passages that teach the authority of Scripture also show the extent of inspiration. If the authority and reliability of Scriptures are complete, Inspiration must extend to all Scripture; It does.

> IF THE AUTHORITY AND RELIABILITY OF SCRIPTURES ARE COMPLETE, INSPIRATION MUST EXTEND TO ALL SCRIPTURE, IT DOES.

There are many passages that make clear the completeness of inspiration and the resulting authority of all Scripture, passages such as Luke 24:25 which says, "O foolish ones, and slow of heart to believe all that the Prophets have spoken." Or Mark 12:24 (AMP), which Jesus, when responding to the Sadducees about the resurrection said, "Is not this where you wander out of the way and go wrong, because you know neither the Scriptures nor the power of God?"

Both Biblical Inspiration and Illumination are the work of the Holy Spirit; He used the personality and talents of those chosen to write the words of the Bible in all its many parts. Because It is God's written Word to men, therefore It is of Divine Authority. While on the other hand, we have the Holy Spirit "Explaining" the Word, giving us a change in thoughts and a new influence from God. Old thoughts come from the old nature, which reveal the sons of disobedience, "lifting and raising themselves against (without) the knowledge of God." New thoughts come from and through Christ, that is, in Christ we bring our thoughts into captivity to the knowledge and obedience of Him Who Loved us.[5]

Illumination comes through meditating on the Word of God, getting His thoughts—His view. The more you get into the Word, the more it gets into you and the more you can begin to see, act, and do, as He would. His Word transforms us. This is why He gave It. "Every Scripture is God-breathed (given by His inspiration) and profitable for instruction, for reproof and conviction of sin, for correction of error and discipline in obedience, *and* for training in righteousness (in holy living, in conformity to God's will in thought, purpose, and action), So that the man of God may be complete and proficient, well fitted and thoroughly equipped for every good work."[6]

Through Illumination and new insight gained from His Word God gives us a change in worldview. Thus, what God has given becomes for us His living, revealing Word. With that said, an interior illumination of the Holy Spirit in the heart and mind of the Believer must complement and balance all other Biblical enlightenment. Otherwise, we have false teachings. Thus, we now see why "the natural, nonspiritual man does not accept or welcome or admit into his heart the gifts and teachings and revelations of the Spirit of God, for they are folly (meaningless nonsense) to him. He is incapable of knowing them *of progressively recognizing, understanding, and becoming better acquainted with them* because they are spiritually discerned, estimated, and appreciated."[7]

In our old view we saw the world through the lenses of a poorly lit soul, blindly following others who themselves lived and walked as captives of darkness. Enlightened, the Believer by the fire of the Holy Spirit has had the spiritual man rekindled to light and life. At once, we realize how we have become His children. Job 32:8 (AMP) says, "But there is *a vital force* a spirit *of intelligence* in man, and the breath of the Almighty gives men understanding."

Thus, illumination is the work of the Holy Spirit."

The witness of the Spirit confirms the Word in us. Jesus said, "But when the Comforter (Counselor, Helper, Advocate, Intercessor, Strengthener, Standby) comes, Whom I will send to you from the Father, the Spirit of Truth Who comes (proceeds) from the Father, He Himself will testify regarding Me.[8]

The Spirit of God has been working to give us a Progressive Revelation of His Will, Plan, and Purposes. Thus, Illumination centers on Jesus Christ our Lord and Savior. For, "while we know that the secret things belong to our God, we also know that the things revealed belong to us and our children forever."[9]

Speaking to the disciples, Jesus said, but when He, the Spirit of Truth (the Truth-giving Spirit) comes, He will guide you into all the Truth (the whole, full Truth).

For He will not speak His own message *with His own authority*; but He will tell whatever He hears *from the Father. He will give the Message that has been given to Him* and He will announce and declare to you the things that are to come *that will happen in the future.*[10]

While the chosen have made the choice to know Him, the rest will not know Him, nor realize the truth, until it is too late. It is the work of the Spirit to confirm the Word in us. He quickens our spirit using the truth that sets men free. Because He confirms our faith, we know that we have not believed in vain. Inwardly, the Spirit is bearing witness with our spirit, even now, that we are, in fact, the children of God.[11]

CHAPTER 11

The Plan Understood

You search and investigate and pore over the Scriptures diligently, because you suppose and trust that you have Eternal Life through them. And these very Scriptures testify about Me![1]

"Enlightened," "Lit up" having your Understanding Opened.

Just as they did then, the many builders today have rejected Jesus as the Christ. Men still oppose Him at every turn, walking in darkness, their eyes closed. While they knew of the prophecies, they could not see the One the prophecies spoke of; the One Who was behind them. Despite all the evidence, they preferred darkness to the Light. They wanted to enter "the Kingdom of Light" on their own terms and not God's. For we read, "But the Pharisees and experts in religious law had rejected God's plan for them, for they had refused John's baptism."[2] As so many do today, "instead of looking for proof that Jesus was the Christ, they revealed the naysayer attitude, by looking for reasons to prove to themselves that He was not." The Pharisees even had disputes among themselves in one case saying, "Are you from Galilee, too? Search the Scriptures and see for yourself—no prophet ever comes from Galilee!"[3] Because of their closed eyes and hardened hearts, they rejected Him. "As Light," He exposed their sins and faults, and while His popularity and credibility grew with the people, theirs eroded. Despite all they saw and heard Jesus do, fear, pride, jealousy, blind rage, and a hardened hatred drove them to do whatever they could to defend their temporal positions, even if

> "INSTEAD OF LOOKING FOR PROOF THAT JESUS WAS THE CHRIST, THEY REVEALED THE NAYSAYER ATTITUDE, BY LOOKING FOR REASONS TO PROVE TO THEMSELVES THAT HE WAS NOT."

it meant plotting evil and committing murder. It has been over two thousand years since the Lord walked on the earth, and "not much has changed." The Will of the Father is that all men might be saved and come to the knowledge of the Truth.[4] His goal is to release us from our fears, that we might become captives of the truth that sets men free.

In the Parable of the two sons, Jesus asked the Jewish leaders a question saying, "But what do you think about this? A man with two sons told the older boy, 'Son, go out and work in the vineyard today.' The son answered, 'No, I won't go,' but later he changed his mind and went anyway. Then the father told the other son, 'You go,' and he said, 'Yes, sir, I will.' But he did not go. Which of the two was obeying his father?" They replied, "The first, of course." Then Jesus explained His meaning: "I assure you; corrupt tax collectors and prostitutes will get into the Kingdom of God before you do. For John the Baptist came and showed you the way to life, and you did not believe him, while tax collectors and prostitutes did. And even when you saw this happening, you refused to turn from your sins and believe him."[5]

The obvious point that Jesus was making here is that while sinners recognized their need for the Savior, the self-righteous (morally upright) leaders did not. Although they saw the example of the repentant tax collectors and prostitutes, they refused to believe and excused themselves. This parable like so many condemns the conduct of the unbeliever. The Scriptures give many such examples of these power struggles common to men in general, and as shown here, the Scribes and Pharisees, who positioned themselves in opposition to the Rule of Christ. It came down to the pursuit of power, a power struggle, and a question of authority. As it is with men today, whether political or religious leaders or would be dictators, theirs was a vain pursuit, forged by temporal mind-sets, seeking temporal power over the things of this present world. The Word says, "The love of money is the root of all evil."[6] Money in this world is a temporal possession, but for many, it becomes an all-consuming obsession, with many equating it with power and possessions. While on the other side of this issue stands pride and fear. Pride brought into confrontation triggers insecurity and fear of loss, loss of power, loss of control or influence. Pride would not allow them to admit their self-deception.

Now at some point in our lives we have all been the victims of lies. For example, as children, grown-ups, and those we trusted told us of Santa Claus and the Easter Bunny, secular symbols designed to compete with Faith in the Birth (Christmas) and Resurrection (Easter) of Jesus Christ. Some would say it was innocent fun; we trusted them of course until we got older and found out otherwise. Now, "When we were children, we spoke, understood, and thought as children; but when we became grown-ups, we should have put childish things away."[7] As grown-ups, we realize that our teachers were not being honest when they told us that man and all Creation on earth came about through this myth called "Evolution." Today, we see those reporting the news, not always reporting the facts, fair and unbiased, some of them have an ax to grind, supporting an agenda, which is less than honest.

Alas, as the saying goes, "If you hear a lie told often enough, you will begin to believe it." Now, "All of this involves various forms of conditioning." Is it any wonder that we believed them? We gave these people our trust not knowing that they, too, were either knowingly or unknowingly deceived, some, all of theirs lives, having conformed, too, and believed in many subtle lies." Some having staked their reputations and lives on what in the end turned out to be false information, which in closer analysis proved to be indefensible. Now as harsh as this may sound, "It is the seed of the serpent" who purposely use subtle deceptions, to lead people astray and away from the truth.

They see no harm in this and wonder in anger and even become offended by Christians who talk of everyone having to stand "in judgment before, the Judge of all men."[8] Nevertheless, the Scriptures contrast their view of angry opposition with the right view. The view that Scripture praises and approves is the one that seeks the truth, no matter where it leads. For example, we see the Bereans having tasted the Word, wanting to know more, and therefore expressing the nobility the Father is looking for. The Scriptures says, "Now the Bereans were of more noble character than the Thessalonians, for they received the Message with great eagerness and examined the Scriptures everyday to see if what Paul said was true.[9]

Illumination comes through examining and studying the Scriptures, while asking the Spirit of God to give you a clear and complete understanding of the Master's Plan. Conversely, people reject the light of truth because of a dark and hardened heart. A sincere study of the Word will set you free from the darkness and put you on the path of light. "Jesus said to the people who believed in Him, 'You are truly My disciples if you keep obeying My teachings. And you will know the truth, and the truth will set you free.'"[10] God wants us free, *He wants to open our eyes and hearts to understand, what He has given,* and He wants us to discover the Truth. He wants to change our outlook, and His Word can do this. But it is up to us to have the courage of conviction to receive it, even when it goes against all that this present world has taught you.

Paul wrote, "Don't copy the behavior and customs of this world, but let God transform you into a new person by changing the way you think. Then you will know what God wants you to do, and you will know how good and pleasing and perfect His will really is."[11]

The power of enlightenment is the light of God *opening your eyes to see the truth in His Word.* It is the power of enlightenment, which gives us the enthusiasm to share His Love and the Message of Salvation with others. This is the power that you see in many newborn Believers, who, in their excitement of learning the Truth, have an eagerness to share "the Message of Hope" with others, having a need to please Him by Faith.

Enlightened Faith is essential to our new life. Enlightened Faith makes life exciting, it changes your worldview, you begin to see old passages in a new light, and this increases your Faith and confidence, giving an even greater thirst and hunger for the truth. This energized Faith is at the center of His Plan for us. "But without Faith it is impossible to please Him and be satisfactory to Him. For whoever would come near to God must necessarily believe that God exist and that He is the rewarder of those who earnestly and diligently seek Him out."[12] Therefore, the goal of His plan is to transform our understanding, to take us from a temporal to an eternal mind-set. To help us come to the life-changing realization that He came to set the captives free. Free from sin, free from Satan, free from the bondage created by death, and the fear of death.

> THEREFORE, THE GOAL OF HIS PLAN IS TO TRANSFORM OUR UNDERSTANDING, TO TAKE US FROM A TEMPORAL TO AN ETERNAL MIND-SET.

Jesus said, "You have your heads in your Bibles constantly because you think you will find Eternal Life there. But you miss the forest for the trees. These Scriptures are all about Me![13]

Listen, in this world we are in a battle for our minds, a spiritual warfare for the souls of men. We are not wrestling against flesh and blood, and the weapons of our warfare are not carnal but mighty in God for pulling down strongholds,[14] these are the "power grips" on the minds of the unsuspecting and unaware. By committing yourself to a program of consistent meditation on the Word, God transforms you into a new person by changing the way you think. His Word will change your perspective, how you see this world, thus equipping you to overcome Satan's lies with God's truths. Then you will know what He wants you to do, then you will see how good and pleasing and how perfect His will really is; you will know. The Apostle Paul wrote, "Finally, brethren, whatever things are *true*, whatever things *are noble*, whatever things *are just*, whatever things *are pure*, whatever things *are lovely*, whatever things *are of good report*, if *there is* any *virtue* and if *there is* anything *praiseworthy—meditate on these things.*"[15]

THE POWER OF MEDITATION

What is Meditation? For the Believer, meditation is the study, contemplation, reflection, and repetitious exposure of his or her mind on "the most precious treasure in the universe," "The Word of God." Meditation is how we program and re-program "our Heart and our Mind."

> *Meditation on the Word of God changes us, thus changing our lives, Psalms 107:20 says, "He sends forth His word, and heals them, and rescues them from the pit and destruction."*

It is true, the Word of God will change you, and this of course is God's Purpose. In Psalms 1:1-3, David said, "Blessed (Happy, fortunate, prosperous and enviable) is the man that Walks and lives Not in the counsel of the ungodly following their advice, their plans and purposes, Nor Stands submissive and inactive in the path where sinners walk, Nor Sits down to relax and rest where the scornful and the mockers gather. But his delight and desire are in the law of the LORD; and on His Law (the precepts, the instructions, and the teachings of God) he habitually meditates (ponders and studies) by day and by night. And he shall be like a tree firmly planted and tended by the streams of water, ready to bring forth its fruit in its season; its leaf also shall not fade or wither; and everything he does shall prosper and come to maturity." Here is a clear contrast between the temporal and eternal, between those who walk, stand, or sit in the vain imaginings of their own mind, and those planted in the Word of God.

The Book of the Law is "the Word," and as we have seen, "Jesus Christ" is also "the Word"; He is the *"Logos,"* the power in, and of, "the Word." In many places, the New Testament writers led by the Holy Spirit took and expounded on what Moses and other Old Testament writers wrote. In the book of Romans, we find many examples of Old Testament statements clarified in the New. In Deuteronomy 30:14, the Word of God says, "But the Word *is* very near you, in your mouth and in your heart, that you may do it." The Apostle Paul, expounding on this verse said, "But what does it say? The Word is near you; it is in your mouth and in your heart," (Deuteronomy 30:14). (That is, the word of faith, which we preach). That if you confess with your mouth, "Jesus is Lord," and believe in your heart that God raised Him from the dead, you will be saved. For with the heart, one believes in righteousness, and with the mouth confession is made unto salvation. For the Scripture says, "Whoever believes on Him will not be put to shame." (Isaiah 28:16). For there is no distinction between Jew and Greek {Gentile}, for the same Lord over all is rich to all who call upon Him.

For "Everyone who calls on the name of the Lord will be saved." (Joel 2:32). How then shall they call on Him in Whom they have not believed? And how shall they believe in Him of Whom they have not heard?

And how shall they hear without a Preacher?

And how shall they Preach unless they are sent?

As it is written, "How beautiful are the feet of those who Preach the Gospel of Peace, who bring glad tidings of Good Things!" (Isaiah 52:7)[16]

Again, "There is power in the Word." Isaiah 55:11 says, "So shall My Word be that goes forth from My Mouth: It shall not return to Me void, but it shall accomplish what I please, and it shall prosper in the thing for which I sent it." The key to understanding and embracing the Plan comes as you behold the Glory of the Lord in His Word, and as you begin to realize that "by His Word," God is transforming you, by faith, from glory to glory.[17] Part of this glory is seeing the glorious Plan that He has for your life.

Total, Whole Person Success

God's Word is Eternal, His Word is the Plan; if you follow the Word, you cannot help being successful, and in the end your prospering will be obvious to all. Following and obeying God's Word is the only way to find true spiritual, whole person success and fulfillment, which is success on a whole person level (spirit, soul, and body)—The "Owner's Manual" gives the standard, He is the Judge. You do not measure success by what you are, but by what you are, compared to what you could have been. You do not measure success by what you have done, but by what you have done, compared to what you could have done.

The Apostle John wrote, "Beloved, I pray that you may prosper in all things and be in health, just as your soul prospers.[18]

"Life and Good," go with our preparation for eternal life, while *"death and evil"* in preparing for a temporal one.

This gets to the heart of the Message in this book, which is "that you might find yourself in Him, and know the Truth of His Word." Ours is a noble pursuit, we are noble people, our Father is the King, we are in pursuit of the Eternal, recognizing all other pursuits lead to compromise with the enemy, and destruction of the soul. The Master's Plan is that we see His calling on our life and pressing on for the prize. That we empowered by His Spirit and encouraged by His Word pursue our calling, realizing there will be rewards. That we through patience, prosper and aim for the goal of becoming and doing what He called and created us to become and do. Sometimes we cannot see the results or benefits of following as He leads us, sometimes we forget or fall into deception, thinking that He is not in control, or has abandoned us. When we get into uncertain circumstances, we sometimes think that He neither sees what is happening, nor is He answering our prayers, but it is always good to remind yourself that He is watching. Rest assured that He both sees and knows, and that He is still working out the Plan, the one He chose for you from before the beginning. *"Know His Word; Know God—No His Word, No God."*

How do you meditate on the Word?

Meditation on God's Word yields knowledge, relevant knowledge. There are several ways to meditate on the Word. The key, however, is to get It out of "the Bible" and engraft It into your soul (your heart). The goal is to memorize and make It apart of you, make it the filter for all your thought processing, filtering everything that comes to you through the Word.

Devotions: Commit yourself to a program of daily devotions, purpose to take in ample quantities of Scripture daily: in the morning, when you get up, during the day, or at night before you go to bed. Make this a priority item; make it something you do on purpose. If you have a busy schedule, readjust it. Be creative, you can read the Word or even listen on audio book, Podcast, or stream.

"Expect resistance," for this is the last thing, your flesh, the world around you and Satan wants you to do.

Word Searches: Do a Scriptural "Word search." Look through your Bible concordance and find "a Word of interest," call it your "Word of the Day."

Now look up each verse that your "Word of the Day" appears in, purposing to get the meaning of that Word in context.

Memorization: Develop a verse-by-verse memorization plan. First find and read a favorite passage of Scripture; next, write out the first letter of each word in the passage. Next, begin to recite the passage over and over, looking only at the first letter of each verse, see the Word as you sequence it in your mind. Continue to do this until you have committed whole sections (chapters) of Scripture to memory. There are other ways to engraft the Word into your heart, and this is something you must do to have complete success and victory. For the more God can get His Word into you, the more it will transform you, and give you the desire to get it out to others. "Pray and ask the LORD to show you how.

By having a planned program for meditating on the Word, you are placing yourself as a student, under the tutelage and training of the Spirit. By knowing the Word of Truth, meditating (thinking on it), hearing it repeatedly in your mind, day, and night, you will be systematically engrafting God's thoughts in your heart (your spirit man, your inner life) and soul. By doing this you allow His Thoughts and Words to become your thoughts and words, as His Word changes you.

God gave us His Word, the Master's Plan to provide us with "a Success Guide for Life." Meditating on the Word is of immeasurable value to every one of us; this is how we get God's truth to overcome Satan's lies. Through faithful study and meditation, God gives us the ability to grow and mature spiritually; this is how He transforms us.

Beloved, God created the first man in, and as, His image. "In Christ," we change, our thoughts, attitude, and opinions of ourselves, by believing what God says about us. Stop and ask yourself, *what do I think about myself,* and then ask, *what does God say about me?* Meditating on the Word will help you STOP agreeing with Satan and his lies and START believing what God has to say about you. God Love's you, He created you on purpose for a purpose, believe it. John 8:32 says, *"And you will know the Truth, and the Truth will set you Free."* Once you catch this truth, it will change the way you see things and give you the resolve to never let the enemies of our soul steal it and sell you something less.

But what is it that we do, when we Meditate on God's Word?

Let us look at some definitions of the word to meditate to gain a better understanding of how we stay in Him and His Word in us.

Meditate (Webster) to be in continuous, contemplative thought, to think about doing something. *Meditate (Roget's Thesaurus)* To think, ponder, or brood over; to muse, mull, and reflect over; to deliberate on, Meditate over; to ruminate, chew over, and digest; to turn over, and revolve in the mind; to give thought or consideration on. This is what He commands us to do with His Word, engraft it in our soul, make it part of our life, for it is our Life. *Jesus said, it is written; "Man shall not live and be upheld and sustained by bread alone, but by every Word that comes forth from the mouth of God.*[19]

Meditating on the Word will give you many advantages, which you cannot even begin to know right now. The Word is like a seed; God gave us His Word that we might search it, much like a Botanist (Plant Scientist) studies, searching out the secrets contained in seeds and plants. Ours is the desire to unlock mysteries contained in the seed of the Word.

It is through the abiding, we in Him and His Word in us, that we are like trees, firmly planted and tended by the streams of water, bringing forth fruit in our appointed season. Our leaves will not fade or wither; and everything that we do will prosper and come to maturity. It is through the abiding, permanently rooted in the Living Water of His Word, the Water nourishing and strengthening the roots of our spiritual life that we grow to be strong. Strong in roots, trunk, and branches with healthy leaves, for these come by continuously, habitually building up our new man our new mind, thus in time we bring forth "the Fruit of Life, the Fruit of the Spirit." Through meditation on the Word, not only do you enter God's power, but also the promises contained in His Word. Here are but a few of the things that knowledge of the Word will equip you to do, God Promises:

You will prosper. (Psalms 1:13).
You will enjoy success. (Joshua 1:8).
Your success will be obvious to all. (1 Timothy 4:15).
You will be filled with joy. (Psalms 63:5, 6).
You will be wiser than all your enemies. (Psalms 119:97, 98).
You will be wiser than all your teachers. (Psalms 119:99,100).
You will have victory over sin. (Psalms 119:9, 11).
You will be able to give wise counsel. (Proverbs 22:17, 18, 21).

Commanding us to "Search the Scriptures," the wisdom of God purposely did this to separate hearers from doers, and nonseekers from seekers. We search His Word to find Him, and we do this by faith. "For we know that *Without Faith it is Impossible to Please Him*: For whoever would come near to God must believe that He exist, and that He is a rewarder of them that diligently and earnestly seek Him out."[20]

> *Let the Word of Christ dwell in you richly in all wisdom, teaching and admonishing one another in Psalms and hymns and spiritual songs, singing with grace in your hearts to the Lord.21*

Part 5 –

Seeing the Plan

CHAPTER 12

A Book in Heaven

There is a Book in Heaven with your name on it, and you are writing the chapters.

And God said, *"Let Us make man in Our Image."*[1] When God (the Trinity) formed the first man He created him in His Image, not that of the angels, nor the apes. But what is the image of God in man? The traditional view has been that man created in God's image held certain moral, ethical, and intellectual abilities, but a more recent view interprets the phrase as also meaning, "Let Us make man **as** Our Image." (The Hebrew preposition in this phrase can be translated to mean either "in" or "*as*").

In addition, the phrase *"according to Our likeness"* draws attention to the *"in or as Our image."* Since God is Spirit,[2] there can be no "Image" or "Likeness" of Him in the normal sense of these words. Indeed, in giving the Ten Commandments, God forbade image making because of its clear ties to the worship of idols.[3]

However, there may be an even greater reason that God outlawed us from making images, even images of God, in that He has already done so! *We are His images, made in His likeness.* While it is true, God made the first Adam in His Image without sin; we also know that Adam's children were born in his image and his likeness and thus born with the sin nature.

When God prepared a body for Christ, *"the Seed of the woman,"* His was a body without the sin nature of the first Adam. His Father was God, not man. Thus, it is the male, and not the female seed, which passes on the sin nature. Nevertheless, even the second Adam did not come in the body of an angel or some other creature; He came in the body of a man.

Now in ancient times, Emperors would command the making of statues in their image and placed them in remote parts of their Empire.

These statues declared that the region was under his power, dominion, and rule. God placed man as a living symbol of Himself on earth to stand for His power, dominion, and rule.

This is the reason God values people so much. In addition, this interpretation fits well, with the command that follows, *"to reign over all that God has made."* God created Adam with intelligence, He brought all the creatures, which He formed out of the ground before Adam, and had Adam name them, which in and of itself is an act of dominion.[4]

God created human beings to reflect His majesty on earth, to have dominion, to rule as His Regents. That is, God created man to rule over His Creation as He would, "wisely and prudently over all that He made." For He said, "let them have dominion over the fish of the sea, over the birds of the air, and over the cattle, over all the earth and over every creeping thing that creeps on the earth. So, God created man in His own image; in the image of God, He created him; male and female He created them. Then God blessed them, and God said to them, "Be fruitful and multiply; fill (refill) the earth and subdue it; have dominion over the fish of the sea, over the birds of the air, and over every living thing that moves on the earth."[5] (See Psalms 8:3-8).

FOR THE RECORD

For the record, God gave man the ability to rule, He gave him dominion over what He Created. God created man and committed a trust to him. With that said, let us shift perspectives, and go a step further; throughout the Word, we find genealogical records. From a bookkeeping perspective, God is an accountant; He keeps records and accounts. Our life here is a stewardship; God holds us accountable and responsible for everything He has committed to our trust. More to the point, why do you think we hear judgment with everyone having to give an account of what he or she has done?

For the record, He knows our thoughts, deeds, even the innermost secrets of our hearts, every lie and misdeed, things that many think are unknown, the Judgments will reveal. For as said earlier, "He even numbered the hairs on our head." Now everyone has an account, a balance sheet, a record of good and evil, both acts of sin and righteousness. For the Believer, Christ has become the deciding factor. He is the deciding factor in everyone's account. He came to do away with the liability of sin. Having Christ is an asset, not having Him a major liability.

From a Genealogical perspective there must be a "Master" family tree in heaven, holding information on everyone ever born, and even conceived into humanity. A family tree, which shows not only who begot whom, from Adam to the last person born in this present Age, but also "the Millennial" Age to come. God not only knows the essentials of everyone born but predetermined when (the time and place in history) that each of us would exist. For the Scripture says, "And He made from one common origin, one source, one blood all nations of men to settle on the face of the earth, having determined their allotted periods of time and the fixed boundaries of their habitation (their settlements, lands, and abodes)."[6]

Again, He Who knows the names of all the stars has kept a genealogical record of the birth, life, and death of every individual ever conceived. We see examples of this in Old Testament books holding just such records or birth order lists. In the New Testament, we find the most important one in Matthew 1:1-17 and Luke 3:23-38.

These trace the bloodline of Christ back through the Old Testament to Abraham and Adam, respectively. Beyond the genealogical list God keeps a record of how well we, as stewards, have managed what He has given us rule over, and what He has entrusted to our care, our time, talents, and temporal possessions. The fact of the matter is this: He has a written book on every individual, a book with family background, history, date of birth and death, and all our life chapters, all in intimate detail. He has done this on each person born. Yes, this includes everyone who has come into existence on the earth, during this present phase of Creation, including you.

Now, at first thought this may seem frightening, but it should come as no surprise that the Father already knows everything about us. God has been around for Eternity, and from all eternity, He has known all His works in intimate detail.

According to the Biblical record, man has been around for close to 6,000 years and is only now on the verge of understanding some of God's mysteries of "the Master Plan for all physical life called, DNA." Men are just beginning to see the secret, inner workings of these miraculous seeds of life called cells, and how, by design, these molecular factories build by dividing and multiplying.

Therefore, as it is with bacteria, so it is with men. Something incredible happens when a bacteria grown in a Petrie dish looks up from under a slide, only to discover that it is under a microscope, always has been. So, it is with men when they discover there are no secrets, God already knows all there is to know about you.

However, when you stop and think about it, it is more serious than this, because it all stands recorded, in our record in heaven, in the mind of God. As you read the verses of Psalm 139 below, try to catch a glimpse not only of the greatness of "His love," but of the infinite number of details that have gone into making His plan for your life. This Psalm, another gem in the royal record, inspired by the Holy Spirit, King David wrote, describing the Love of the Father, while revealing three of His greatest qualities to us:

(1) His knowledge of all things—His Omniscience
(2) His presence everywhere—His Omnipresence
(3) His power forming and shaping us—His Omnipotence
(4) His awesome and matchless Love

As we look at God's work in the continuing miracle of life, please consider and meditate on what David wrote.

OMNISCIENCE

O LORD, You have searched me and known me. You know my sitting down and my rising up; You understand my thought afar off. You understand my path and my lying down and are acquainted with all my ways. For there is not a word on my tongue, but behold, O LORD, You know it altogether. You have hedged me behind and before and laid Your hand upon me. Such knowledge is too wonderful for me; It is to high; I cannot reach it.[7]

Omniscience describes His knowledge, "He knows all there is to know about us." He knows all the intimate details of your life—again, this may be a fearful thought at first, but it is true. He knows where you have been and where you are going; He knows what you are thinking and what you are going to say, even before you do. This also explains His providential care for Creation, and as His workmanship, how He leads you and I to fulfill the Faith-Vision, which He has for us. You are a living Faith-Vision of the Almighty; what you do with the vision is in your hands, it is up to you. You can follow Him and His Word, allowing Him to shape and mold you into the Vision that He has for you. On the other hand, you can trash it and throw it away; living life your way, on your terms, your conditions; but know this, know that He will hold each of us accountable for what we have done. He will require an accounting of our works, words, and deeds, namely, what we have done with His Word. Again, His Plan is for us to see the Truth, and live a life that glorifies Him, here on earth, as you seek His will and follow His calling. He brings about those events that work to shape and mold us into the image of His Son, "For the ways of man are before the eyes of the LORD, and He ponders all his paths." Mark well that God does not miss a move you make; He is aware of every step you take.[8]

"The eyes of the LORD keep guard over knowledge and him who has it, but He overthrows the words of the treacherous."[9]

OMNIPRESENCE

Where can I go from Your Spirit? Or where can I flee from Your presence? If I ascend into Heaven, You are there; If I make my bed in Hell, behold, You are there. If I take the wings of the morning, and dwell in the uttermost parts of the sea, even there Your hand shall lead me, and Your right hand shall hold me. If I say, "Surely the darkness shall cover me," Even the night shall be light about me; Indeed, the darkness shall not hide from You, But the night shines as the day; The darkness and the light are both alike to You.[10]

Omnipresence describes where He is, "God is everywhere, and in every time, He sees it all." You cannot hide from His Love. Even if we wanted to, there is nowhere in Creation that we can go to hide from His presence. Job 34:21 says, "For *God's* eyes are upon the ways of a man, and He sees all his steps." There is nothing hidden from His sight for, "the eyes of the LORD are in every place, keeping watch on the evil and the good."[11] "The eyes of the Lord watch over those who do right, and His ears are open to their prayers. But the Lord turns His face against those who do evil."[12] He knows when we are suffering, and responds to our cries for help, He stands opposed to all who do not follow in His path of righteousness.

For *"there is no creature hidden from His sight, but all things are naked and open to the eyes of Him to Whom we must give account.*[13]

OMNIPOTENCE

For You formed my inward parts; You covered me in my mother's womb. I will praise You, for I am fearfully and wonderfully made; Marvelous are Your works; And that my soul knows very well. My frame was not hidden from You, when I was made in secret, and skillfully wrought in the lowest parts of the earth. Your eyes saw my substance, being yet unformed; and in Your book they all were written, the days fashioned for me, when yet there was none of them. How precious also are Your thoughts to me, O God! How great is the sum of them! If I should count them, they are more in number than the sand: When I awake, I am still with You.[14]

Omnipotence describes His power, "God is all-powerful." All matter and energy are under His control; all power is in His hands. His power formed each one of us in the womb. Job said, "You guided my conception and formed me in the *womb*."[15] God told Jeremiah, "Before I formed you in the *womb* I knew you; before you were born I sanctified you; I ordained you a prophet to the nations."[16] When the Apostle Paul came to realize God's hand over his life, even before his birth, he recounted the following in his testimony about his persecution of the Church in her infancy, when he says, "But then something happened! For it pleased God in His kindness to choose me and call me, *even before I was born!* What undeserved mercy! Then He revealed His Son to me so that I could proclaim the Good News about Jesus to the Gentiles."[17]

This is all powerful information when you consider just how well our heavenly Father knows us. How intimately aware He is of all our ways. "The Father loves us so much, He knows us intimately, and it's a comforting thought to know that no matter where you are, His Spirit and Presence is only a call in prayer away." For, "the eyes of the LORD are upon the righteous, and His ears are open unto their cry." [18] In Part 6, "Intelligent Designs," we will uncover more evidence on just how much detail went into making our bodies. Discoveries in DNA research are revealing even greater levels of complexity of this mystery called life. We can see His love in the growth and development (the seed of physical life), which each of us has undergone in the womb. You can also look and reflect upon all that He chose for you outside the womb for example, He chose your:

Parents… Your natural father and mother
Time of your birth… In history; year, month, day, even the hour
Background… Ethnic and racial
National heritage… Nation or country of your birth
Gender… Male or female
Birth order in the family… First, second, third child
Brothers and sisters… Number and gender of your siblings

Physical features and appearance… He designed all your facial features, the size, and shape of your ears, nose, and mouth, the color of your eyes, and the texture of your hair

He is aware of your physical, mental, and emotional abilities; He knows your age, and even the time when you will leave this earthy house of clay.

Behold, children are a heritage from the LORD, The fruit of the womb is a reward.[19]

Yet with all that He has done, why is it that so many mistakenly blame God for the works of sinful man.

DOWN MEMORY LANE

Broken promises, abusive relationships, unresolved conflicts, unforgiveness, and bitterness have caused much pain, and left many with open, festering, and unhealed wounds. Sin is still in the world and multitudes are suffering its effects. The Devil and his agents are busily wreaking havoc, destruction, and ruin in the lives of many. Families and individuals fail because of ignorance, not knowing and therefore not showing God's love; they pass on sinful behaviors and generational curses, one generation to the next. Proving the truth that *"hurting people, hurt people"* and *"people perish for lack of knowledge."*

Satan uses people's own lack of knowledge and understanding against them to harm both them and the ones they claim to love. These people lack both knowledge of the Laws of God and understanding of the rules of life. Sadly, there are far too many wounded by the fiery darts of an unsuspected enemy, leaving many angry, bitter, and hardened. Without the power to forgive, they turn inward, and in so doing turn against God.

They say things like, *"How could a loving God have allowed this to happen,"* or *"If God really cared, He wouldn't have allowed this to happen to me."* Knowing there will be consequences, Satan and his demons are much too clever to mount a direct assault on Believers without asking for and getting permission. Satan asked for permission to test Peter to sift him as wheat.[20] God gave him permission to test Job.[21] "The Accuser" knows in the Judgment God will condemn those who abused and neglected believers, for Jesus said, "When you did it to one of the least of these my brothers and sisters, you did it to Me!" He was of course talking about His Body, the Church.[22]

Instead of a direct assault, Satan and his host work through the lust of the flesh, the lust of the eyes and the pride of life.[23] Remember, we do not wrestle (fight) against flesh and blood, our real battle is not against human beings, be they Liberals Secularist, Atheist, Agnostics, or even fake Christians. Our real conflict is against forces of darkness who through skillful manipulation use the unsuspecting and unaware, those who are fully under their sway, and power, those held captive to the carnal (temporal) nature. They attack and seduce people with unholy thoughts and impulses, to bring about conditions and circumstances designed to foment disagreement, strife, conflict, and division, all of which put people "on the out" with one another. Mature Believers, "those who by reason of use have their senses exercised to discern both good and evil,"[24] can see how the enemy works and thus practice the power of forgiveness. Paul revealed the immaturity in Believers when he said, "And I, brethren, could not speak to you as to spiritual people but as to carnal, as to babes in Christ. I fed you with milk and not with solid food; for until now you were not able to receive it, and even now you are still not able; for you are still carnal. For where there are envy, strife, and divisions among you, are you not carnal and behaving like mere men?"[25] Instead of seeing the wickedness of the sinful nature, the immature and unbelieving blame God for the evil created by the enemies' wiles and schemes. All of this leads them to make, but not see, the consequences of poor choices, either their own or those of others. The enemy's goal is to keep people outside the will of God, and hit them with fiery darts,[26] to shake and destroy any faith they might have had. *The enemy cannot use our humility; he can only use our anger.* Thus, in anger he causes many to focus on wounds, which germinate into seeds of mistrust with many speaking evil and in malice of vengeance, because they do not know the ways and laws of God. Paralyzed, they focus on an anger-filled past. In time, their heart grows cold and hard, and a root of bitter hatred and unforgiveness springs up within, producing a borderline insanity thus, defiling any hope,[27] unless God in someway intervenes.

Thus, there is even more reason to strive and encourage other believers to strive for maturity. For "Then we will no longer be like children, forever changing our minds about what we believe because someone has told us something different or because someone has cleverly lied to us and made the lie sound like the truth. Instead, we will hold to the truth in love, becoming increasingly in every way like Christ, Who is the head of His body, the Church."[28]

FORGIVENESS

*T*he story of the Unforgiving Debtor shows what happens when believers do not forgive one another of their sins and trespasses. The Scripture says, "Then Peter came to him and asked, "Lord, how often should I forgive someone who sins against me? Seven times?"

"No!" Jesus replied, "seventy times seven!"

"For this reason, the Kingdom of Heaven can be compared to a king who decided to bring his accounts up to date with servants who had borrowed money from him. In the process, one of his debtors was brought in who owed him millions of dollars. He could not pay, so the king ordered that he, his wife, his children, and everything he had to be sold to pay the debt. But the man fell before the king and begged him, 'Oh, sir, be patient with me, and I will pay it all.' Then the king was filled with pity for him, and he released him and forgave his debt.

"But when the man left the king, he went to a fellow servant who owed him a few thousand dollars. He grabbed him by the throat and demanded instant payment. His fellow servant fell before him and begged for a little more time. 'Be patient and I will pay it,' he pleaded."

But his creditor would not wait. He had the man arrested and jailed until the debt could be paid in full. "When some of the other servants saw this, they were upset. They went to the king and told him what had happened. Then the king called in the man he had forgiven and said, 'You evil servant! I forgave you that tremendous debt because you pleaded with me. Shouldn't you have mercy on your fellow servant, just as I had mercy on you?' Then the angry king sent the man to prison until he had paid every penny. That is what My heavenly Father will do to you if you refuse to forgive your brothers and sisters in your heart."[29]

Remember, "Above all things have intense and unfailing love for one another, for love covers a multitude of sins it forgives and disregards the offenses of others."[30]

IT'S ABOUT GRACE

When people come to know the Truth, the plans, schemes and wiles of the enemy, and the power of forgiveness, everything changes. God uses broken people. It is only by grace and the tender mercies of God that we come to recognize these sins as snares and traps, weights of the enemy. Assaults designed to drown souls in a sea of self-pity, hopelessness, and despair; "This is not of God."

Never sacrifice your faith, no matter what clever plan the enemy uses against you; always "trust in God." Remember, Paul warned us not to look at things according to there outer appearance, he also said, "Although we walk in the flesh, we do not war according to the flesh. For the weapons of our warfare are not carnal but mighty in God for pulling down strongholds, casting down arguments and every high thing that exalts itself against the knowledge of God, bringing every thought into captivity to the obedience of Christ, and being ready to punish all disobedience when your obedience is fulfilled."[31]

The enemy's goal is to steal, kill, and destroy. God's Plan is to help us see the power of forgiveness for others, to heal us from sin, and restore us to right relationship with Him, to make us whole. The lives of Job and Joseph, son of Jacob, explain the trials and tests of this life all too well. Job said, "Though He slay me, yet will I trust Him."[32] At the end of his trial having passed the test, God blessed him with a double part of all the enemy had taken.

While, at the end of his trials, Joseph said to his brothers, "You meant evil against me; *but* God meant it for good, to bring it about *as it is* this day, to save many people alive."[33]

God says, "Vengeance is Mine, I will repay."[34]

WE ARE GOD'S CHILDREN

From the beginning, when God gave Adam dominion, His Plan has been to create a Nation of Priest and Kings. As Believers, "We are a chosen generation, a Royal Priesthood, a Holy Nation, His own special people, that you may proclaim the praises of Him Who called you out of darkness into His marvelous light."[35] We are a people in transition, transitioning from walking in the flesh, to walking in the Spirit. Our Father is the Sovereign One, the King of all Creation. Yet many Believers suffer from a crisis of identity. Instead of living on earth with knowledge of the inheritance that awaits us and working to increase our reward, on our journey home far too many see this present Age and life as the real life, thinking, *"This is It."* Spiritually speaking, they live as vagabonds and paupers, not knowing that our Heavenly Father longs for them to know His Will and Plan for their lives *"right now,"* on this side of the journey. His desire is that they would realize that we are here on probation, to be tried and tested, to grow, develop, and mature to perfect our nature into the image of His Son, our Creator the Lord Jesus Christ. We are the adopted children of the King.[36]

"For He has not put the world to come, of which we speak, in subjection to angels. But one testified in a certain place, saying:

"What is man that You are mindful of him, Or the son of man that You take care of him? You have made him a little lower than the angels; You have crowned him with glory and honor And set him over the works of Your hands. You have put all things in subjection under his feet."

For in that He put all in subjection under him, He left nothing that is not put under him. But now we do not yet see all the things put under him. But we see Jesus, who was made a little lower than the angels, for the suffering of death crowned with glory and honor, that He, by the grace of God, might taste death for everyone.

For it was fitting for Him, for whom are all things and by whom are all things, in bringing many sons to glory, to make the captain of their salvation perfect through sufferings. For both He who sanctifies and those who are sanctified are all of one, for which reason He is not ashamed to call them brethren, saying:

"I will declare Your name to My brethren; In the midst of the assembly, I will sing praise to You."

And again:

"I will put My trust in Him."

And again:

"Here am I and the children whom God has given Me."

Inasmuch then as the children have partaken of flesh and blood, He Himself likewise shared in the same, that through death He might destroy him who had the power of death, that is, the devil, and release those who through fear of death were all their lifetime subject to bondage. For indeed He does not give aid to angels, but He does give aid to the Seed of Abraham. Therefore, in all things He had to be made like His brethren, that He might be a merciful and faithful High Priest in things about God, to make propitiation for the sins of the people. For in that He Himself has suffered, being tempted, He is able to aid those who are tempted.[37]

In Christ, Our Father has made us brothers and sisters "of Christ." He helps us see this life as a temporary assignment and temporal arrangement, on probation. While we are here, God uses our lives, to bring about our part in His Plan, with the goal of bringing us to our reward, our real future, and eternal life with Him. He loves you so much, He sees and knows your pains, He knows when and what you have gone through, and how your love has covered a multitude of sins. He knows all about your trials and heartaches, He watches, He sees your tears. He has never left, nor abandoned you; you have learned to trust Him, and He has carried you through. Again, the Scriptures says, because Christ, "*In His humanity* has suffered in being tempted (tested and tried), He is able *immediately* to run to the cry of (assist, relieve) those who are being tempted and tested and tried *and who therefore are being exposed to suffering.*"[38] The Psalmist says, "You keep track of all my sorrows. You have collected all my tears in Your bottle. You have recorded each one in your book."[39] His love for His children is closer than the love of our earthly father and mother, the Word says, "Even if my father and mother abandon me, the LORD will hold me close."[40]

WHO IS THE TRUE FAMILY OF JESUS?

Once Jesus was speaking to a crowd, and His mother and brothers were outside wanting to talk with Him. Someone told Jesus, "Your mother and your brothers are outside, and they want to speak to you." Jesus asked, "Who is My mother? Who are My brothers?" Then He pointed to His disciples and said, "These are My mother and brothers. Anyone who does the will of My Father in heaven is My brother and sister and mother!" [41] Are you praying for the Salvation of your earthly family? The family of heaven does not consist of flesh and blood, but is a spiritual family of believers, those who do the Will of the Father. While family bonds are strong, they are a part of our natural (temporal) life, not the new eternal one.

Just as Satan in the garden used the snake, throughout the generations he has used men and women who are his seed in nature. Not everyone in our earthly family is a part of our heavenly family; they must be born again, too. Remember, "Jesus said a man's enemies will be those of his own household."

CHRIST BRINGS DIVISION

"Do not imagine that I came to bring peace to the earth! No, I came to bring a sword. I have come to set a man against his father, and a daughter against her mother, and a daughter-in-law against her mother-in-law. Your enemies will be right in your own household! If you love your father or mother more than you love Me, you are not worthy of being Mine; or if you love your son or daughter more than Me, you are not worthy of being Mine. If you refuse to take up your cross and follow Me, you are not worthy of being Mine. If you cling to your life, you will lose it; but if you give it up for Me, you will find it."[42] The goal is to follow Him, not the world; walk as a new Creation, in the Spirit and not after the flesh. When it comes to your earthly family, pray for them.

Trust in God's foreknowledge and providential care for you. He does not lie.

BOOKS WILL BE OPENED

In the judgment, God will open other books and "The Book of Life." He has your book (your biography) in heaven, the one that gives every intimate detail about you and your present life here on the earth. Every chapter and page, every word written in Heaven; remember, God knows more about us than just the numbered shafts of hair on our head. He foreknew the names of every person written in "the Lamb's Book of Life," and those who were not. That is right, right now, there is a book in Heaven that holds the names of all who would become "the seed and offspring of God." In this book, you will not find the names of the seed and offspring of the serpent (the snake). We know the next major event on the prophetic calendar is the catching away, "the Rapture" of the Church, or *"the Ekklesia,"* meaning, *"the Called-Out ones."*

During the Tribulation, "All those on the earth will worship the beast—all whose names have not been written in the book of life belonging to the Lamb that was slain from the Creation of the world."[43] For those who understand, this is what makes the fear of the LORD so real. Through knowledge of prophecy, and many anti-Christian movements going on around the world, we can see last day's events aligning themselves to unfold. Thus, the Word is real, for those who know that men must stand before one of the two Judgments: The first, "the Judgment seat of Christ," is for Believers for rewards. Whereas the second, "the Great White Throne Judgment," is for unbelievers and those who have never heard the Gospels, for they, too, will have to give an account of their works and deeds. For the righteous, this is what causes men to turn from evil. Sadly, those who do not understand do not know that every word, act, and deed stand recorded in heaven.

Scripture says, "From the time the world was created, people have seen the earth and sky and all that God made. They can clearly see His invisible qualities—His Eternal Power and Divine Nature. So, they have no excuse whatsoever for not knowing God.[44]

People go through this life blind, oblivious to God, oblivious to His judgments. When Believers stand before Him, we will see a review of our life on earth. Remember and remind yourself as you begin to write new chapters in a new life that He knows your life-story from beginning to end. You are a living Faith-Vision of the Almighty God, the Creator. Just as He formed all the details and features of your physical frame inside your mother's womb, God has dedicated Himself to continuing the work of making you complete in this life. His work and purpose have been to form the character and personality of your inner man into that of His only begotten Son, the Holy One and source of "True Righteousness," the Lord Jesus Christ. "For we are God's *Own* handiwork (His workmanship), re-created in Christ Jesus, *born anew* that we may do those good works which God predestined (planned beforehand) for us *taking paths which He prepared ahead of time*, that we should walk in them *living the good life which He prearranged and made ready for us to live."*[45] This is the life, life directed by the Holy Spirit, a life, which strives for righteous living. It should be clear from the Scriptures that God is constantly thinking of you, wanting to see you become all that He meant you to be, for the life to come. We are in training, running a race; God gave the Word, "the Owner's manual," to us for this precise reason. As it says, "All Scripture is given by inspiration of God, and is profitable for doctrine, for reproof, for correction, for instruction in Righteousness, that the man of God may be complete, thoroughly equipped for every good work."[46]

> "WHEN BELIEVERS STAND BEFORE HIM, WE WILL SEE A REVIEW OF OUR LIFE ON EARTH."

The truth here is that the person who knows the Word, both understanding and applying it, never loses his or her way. This is the Work of God; all around the World He is perfecting the body. Paul said, "And I am convinced and sure of this very thing, that He Who began a good work in you will continue until the day of Jesus Christ *right up to the time of His return*, developing *that good work* and perfecting and bringing it to full completion in you." [47] God has given us this stage of life for developing our spirit man. Here on earth, we are on probation, and our good works consist of God developing our inner man's character, attitude, and disposition, into that of His Son. The Father does this, as we do His Work and Will. Therefore, He says to us, "Let your character or moral disposition be free from love of money including greed, avarice, lust, and craving for earthly possessions and be satisfied with your present circumstances and with what you have; for He, God Himself has said, I will not in any way fail you nor give you up nor leave you without support."[48] Of course, temporal minded, prosperity preachers would disagree with all of this. The Psalmist says, "I have been young, and now am old; yet I have not seen the righteous forsaken, nor his seed (descendants) begging bread."[49] It all comes down to trust, "Do you trust in the LORD with all your heart? Are you leaning on Him for His understanding, and acknowledging Him in all your ways? Are you allowing Him to direct your paths?"[50]

"Some have their Mansions on earth, others, in heaven."

MORE ON DIVINE APPOINTMENTS

Because of the Creator's interest and involvement in His Creation, much of what happens to us in this life goes beyond mere coincidence. For Believers, these events involve more than mere chance meetings or accidental happenings. As we experience these foreordained meetings, happenings, and events, we come to recognize them as appointments orchestrated by heaven, which reveal our Father's intervention into our lives and His Creation.

As we said in Chapter 6, "Divine Appointments" are representative of those milestones and events, which mark the climax, the beginning, or end of a life chapter in our book already written in heaven. The Scriptures make it clear; there is a time and season for every purpose under heaven. However, the idea of God deciding those times, seasons, and life events by "Divine Appointment" is not that well known. However, knowing both this, and the goal of the Plan, gives us greater insight, helping us walk into the future with assurance. In Christ, we have seen His ordained interventions into His Creation. Therefore, we should never underestimate the incalculable power and benefits of our prayers. Many divine appointments are a direct response to His answering our prayers. Prayers are our part in helping move the Plan forward. In Prayer we are saying we want what God wants. Prayer is God's Will. While other appointments in life come about through His foreordained, purposeful intervention into the lives of His people, in the chain of His fulfilling, unfulfilled promises in His Word.

Thus, the characteristics of divine appointments fall into two categories: answered Prayer and God fulfilling His Word. Divine Appointments are signs; like beacons along the way lighting our path. They give comfort, we are not alone; they give hope, He has not abandoned us; and assurance that we are on the right path, the path of life. The LORD says, *"I will not, I will* not, *I will* not in any degree leave you helpless nor forsake nor let *you* down! *Assuredly not!* So, we take comfort and are encouraged and confidently and boldly say: The LORD is my Helper; I will not be seized with alarm *I will not fear or dread or be terrified.* What can man do to me?"[51]

Have Faith in God, trust Him to finish in you what He started in Christ. "And therefore, the Lord *earnestly* waits *expecting, looking, and longing* to be gracious to you; and therefore, He lifts Himself up, that He may have mercy on you and show loving-kindness to you. For the LORD is a God of justice. Blessed (happy, fortunate, to be envied) are all those who *earnestly* wait for Him, who expect and look and long for Him *for His victory, His favor, His love, His peace, His joy, and His matchless, unbroken companionship.*"[52] This is the victory over the flesh, the world, and Satan; this is the mystery of walking in the new life. We have no greater purpose than to wait for Him, as we run this race, as we write what He has written, this is His Master Plan for us. "But they that wait upon the LORD shall renew their strength; they shall mount up with wings like eagles, they shall run and not be weary, they shall walk and not faint." [53]

CHAPTER 13

This Journey called Life

Life is here, and hereafter, what you do here will decide what you will be doing hereafter.

OUR JOURNEY THROUGH THIS WORLD IS ONE OF FAITH.

Each of us began this life in the flesh, and, at some point, God touched our heart. "Suddenly," we recognized the need for a change, a new life; this led us to the new birth. We accepted Christ in our heart, and we were born again. Those who persisted in Faith eventually came to the realization that we are in a race, competing against self. By Faith, following the goal of His high calling, "focusing on Him, running for a prize."[1]

WHAT IS ETERNAL LIFE?

"Eternal Life, Everlasting Life, Living Forever; Infinity, Never Ending," try as you might to grasp the idea or significance of these words and you will always fall short. God planted this idea of Eternal Life, and the wish to live forever, within our hearts. However, it is obvious in our present state, and to our natural senses, that there is a veil, over and around us, which takes any conception of it just out of reach. For, while our souls are eternal, these fleshly bodies are not. The evidence says these bodies get old and die; our natural senses tell us that it is just not possible, and with all the pain, trials, and sufferings in life, who would want to live forever? But the truth of God's Word paints a different picture. While it is true that we are all going to die in this life, the question becomes, "Then what." God's Word gives the only reasonable answer for both the Believer and Unbeliever; and that answer leaves us with a case of extremes, both in purpose and direction. If you believe and receive Christ, you will go one way; if you do not, you will go the other. The God Who is Love has eternal life and wants to share it with us.

Jesus is the way, and no one can come to the Father except through Him.[2] In the Master Plan, God gives us the secret of "The Journey to Eternal Life." For the believer, this present earth is not our home; this is not our world; as pilgrims and strangers, we are just passing through." As we said, God already knows about our journey and life here on earth, the book of our life here on earth, already written in Heaven. "Born again," our name written in the Lamb's Book of Life. Jesus Christ is alive in Heaven right now and He will come again to receive His own from the earth. While He is away, He called us to continue in His service. For He said, "If any man serves Me, let him follow Me; and where I Am, there shall also My servant be: if any man serves Me, him will My Father honor."[3] We serve Him by growing to be like Him.

When the Master returns, He will honor many servants, but those who rejected Him, He will condemn.

God chose the Apostle Paul to reveal the Message of Hope to those predestined for Eternal Life. It was his vast knowledge of the Old Testament, which allowed God to use him mightily to give many revelations of the Masters Plan to the Church.

He understood the Plan and took full advantage of his commission to spread the Gospel, the "Good News" of Eternal Life, found only in Christ. He prayed for and wrote many letters to the Church, many of which he and others planted, often wishing to revisit them and see their progress. However, all of this happened "after" his transformation on the road to Damascus. There he experienced a Significant Emotional Event (S.E.E.); he had a "sudden" encounter with the resurrected Christ, which convinced him that what he had fought against was in fact the truth, the truth about Jesus Christ, the Resurrection, and Eternal Life. *The Holy Spirit opened his understanding.* "On the road to Damascus; *God blinded him, to open his eyes."* But Paul is not alone, for over the years many disciples, Apostles, Prophets, Evangelist, and Pastor-Teachers have also given their lives to the service of spreading the Gospel, the Good News of Eternal Life, "the Message of Jesus Christ." Now we have the same task of sharing "the Good News." A Message, which those who belong to and have committed themselves to this world intensely hate and bitterly oppose (many of them do not even know why). The Message is the truth of what this life is all about, as it exposes the conflict between the children of Light and children of Darkness. This is the Message we joyfully proclaim.

LIFE, "A THREEFOLD JOURNEY"

So, what is Eternal Life? As believers, we understand that God created us all. We also understand that "In Christ" God has been carrying us through this life, which is the second stage of a Journey, which began at conception and will end in eternity, or from this life to new life.

From Birth to Life

Again, look at it this way; for us life is a threefold Journey. The first stage of the journey began at conception and continued with our physical development in our mother's womb; that stage ended with our deliverance into this world of "the second stage." By analogy, this is comparable to the nation of Israel in the Old Testament. As a people, the Nation grew and developed in the womb of Egypt, with the sign of their birth being "the Passover." As the people of God, they had a small beginning, but grew bigger and stronger, until the day of their physical deliverance out of Egypt as a nation. Thus, we can compare this to the physical development phase, in which we get these sheaths, these encasings for our soul. By comparison, the first stage of our journey is from the womb to this world. From the time of our conception, our toiling and growing in the womb, until the time of our birth, our delivery into this world of our temporal existence.

The second stage began on the day of our birth, having entered this temporal life, which will continue until our death. This stage of the journey is comparable to the Passover, from the day that Israel became an independent Nation, until it came time to enter the Promised Land. Israel having left the womb of Egypt, headed out for the Promised Land. However, just as it was for them, so it is for us; there must be a rebirth, a change in nature, and way of thinking, a coming to the truth. This comes about through planting the seed of God's Word. They embarked on a journey of Faith, which required them to let go of the mind-set inherent to Egypt, "the world." They all passed through the Red Sea, which for them was a sign of baptism.[4] This for us is our immersion into the new life in Christ.

Now, because of the sin of unbelief the first generation, representative of the old nature, the old man, died in the wilderness. It was only the second generation, representative of the born again, the new nature, the new man that

> HERE AND NOW, IS WHERE WE MATURE AND BRING FORTH FRUIT. HERE WE HAVE OPPORTUNITY TO PREPARE FOR OUR ROLE AND PLACE IN THE KINGDOM.

God allowed entry into the Land of Promise. In the Wilderness, they had been on probation, undergoing trial and testing. God used their trials and personal testimonies to teach us, and to show those who had the faith to trust Him. He used their Faith to decide the worthiness of those going in and taking possession of the Land of Promise, which for us is the New Jerusalem, the city of God. The third stage of this journey is from this life to Eternity, to the New Life, and New Jerusalem. We traveled the first stage of life from the womb, the place of our physical development, there fitted with a body, which God prepared for our journey here on earth. We entered this, the second stage of life, where we develop our souls, our spirit man into a new creation. Here and now is where we mature and bring fruit forth. Here we can prepare for our role and place in the kingdom. Consider the loss of those who do not know, who do not have a clue, those who have never looked beyond this world, to Eternal Life and things to come. Then God will give us a body suitable to the transformed soul and spirit, developed in this life, which will live and last forever.

WHOSE REPORT ARE YOU GONNA BELIEVE!

Let us look at this life from another point of view. In the book of Numbers (Chapters 13 and 14), we have the account of the nation Israel succumbing to fear over faith. Even after seeing all that God had brought them through, after years of bondage and slavery at the hand of Pharaoh in Egypt. They had a choice to make.

First, He sent them a deliverer, *"Moses."* Second, by a strong hand, He sent great plagues on Egypt to secure their release. Third, by a strong east wind, He parted the Red Sea so they might pass through on dry land, but He drowned Pharaoh's army. Fourth, they were in the wilderness covered by His hand of protection, a pillar of cloud by day, and fire by night, while in route to the Promised Land. When they came to the borders of the Promise Land, they sent twelve spies to scout out the land.

After forty days, the twelve returned with fruit from the land and words declaring the riches of this land that flowed with milk and honey. Prompted by fear, because the inhabitants were strong and their cities fortified; fear gripped ten of the spies, who expressed sentiments, which stole the hope and courage of the people and filled their hearts with fear. Doubt crept in and cast a long shadow of discouragement over the whole congregation.

However, the two faithful spies (Joshua and Caleb) brought a favorable report; they stood up and boldly reminded the people, God had promised the land to them. Caleb said, "Let us go up at once, and take possession," declaring, "For we are well able to overcome it." Because of their unbelief, God turned the nation around and led them back into the wilderness to wander for forty years until everyone in that generation perished, the exceptions, Joshua, Caleb, and Moses.

Life is a test of faith; "Christ is the Answer," Pass, or fail.

During this, our wilderness phase of the journey, the first generation, representative of "Unbelievers," the old nature and the old man, will die in the wilderness of this world. The second generation, representative of "Believers," the new nature and the new man, believed God and are looking forward to the third stage, the stage beyond the wilderness of this life, to the life to come. For the believer, the born again, "the Rapture," will open the door to the life to come.

Have Faith in God, trust Him to bring you out of this wilderness of trial and temptation, by His power, and into our Promised Land, "give in to hope—never give in to fear." Have FAITH over FEAR— Faith is, "Fervently Abiding In The Hope, overcoming False Evidence Appearing Real."

Thus, God's work of creating man was twofold. The first consisted of creating the earthy man, God's breath giving life to the soil of the earth; the second consist of transforming earthborn man into a new, heavenly creation. Transforming him, on the inside here on earth, and the outside, giving him a new body at "the Rapture."

The Scriptures tell us, "The first man, Adam, became a living person." But the last Adam—that is, Christ—is a life-giving Spirit. What came first was the natural body, then the spiritual body comes later. Adam, the first man, was made from the dust of the earth, while Christ, the second man, came from heaven. Every human being has an earthly body just like Adam's, but our heavenly bodies will be just like Christ's. Just as we are now like Adam, the man of the earth, so we will someday be like Christ, the man from heaven. What I am saying, dear brothers and sisters, is that flesh and blood cannot inherit the Kingdom of God. These perishable bodies of ours are not able to live forever. But let me tell you a wonderful secret God has revealed to us. Not all of us will die, but we will all be transformed. It will happen in a moment, in the blinking of an eye, when the last trumpet is blown. For when the trumpet sounds, the Christians who have died will be raised with transformed bodies. And then we who are living will be transformed so that we will never die. For our perishable earthly bodies must be transformed into heavenly bodies that will never die.

When this happens—when our perishable earthly bodies have been transformed into heavenly bodies that will never die—then at last the Scriptures will come true:

"Death is swallowed up in victory.
O death, where is your victory?
O death, where is your sting?"

For sin is the sting that results in death, and the law gives sin its power. How we thank God, Who gives us victory over sin and death through Jesus Christ our Lord! So, my dear brothers and sisters, be strong and steady, always enthusiastic about the Lord's work, for you know that nothing you do for the Lord is ever useless. ⁵ Again, as "the Resurrection and the Life," when He returns for His Church, He will raise and give Eternal Life to His people. Then He will be "the Resurrection" for those who have died and "the Life" for those who have not. All this wonderful truth runs counter to the many theories of man's origin, and future, which permeate the minds of the temporal-minded (the unregenerate, unbelieving). Those, whose ideas of our origin, our condition, purpose for our existence and end, have their origin, in the imaginations of men. Listen, God is Good, Satan is Evil, and human beings will have one of these two natures. All people who enter the second stage of the Journey must choose. "If you're born twice, you will die once, maybe; if you're born once, you will die twice." It is yours to lose. First the natural, then the spiritual; God's purpose is to bring souls into this world and then, into the Kingdom. Which direction will you choose? *"Whose report are you gonna believe!"*

> *We decide our destiny on this side of the journey, so aim high, set your affection on things above, not on the things of the earth.*

Like all the other Apostles, *Paul knew the power of enlightenment having had his own eyes opened.* Therefore, his constant prayer for the Church of Ephesus was that their eyes be flooded with light so they could see His glorious Plan; this prayer we extend to you. He said, "Ever since I first heard of your strong faith in the Lord Jesus and your love for Christians everywhere, I have never stopped thanking God for you. I pray for you constantly, asking God, the glorious Father of our Lord Jesus Christ, to give you spiritual wisdom and understanding, so that you might grow in your knowledge of God. "I pray that your hearts will be flooded with light so that you can understand the wonderful future He has promised to those He called. I want you to realize what a rich and glorious inheritance He has given to His people. I pray that you will begin to understand the incredible greatness of His power for us who believe Him. This same mighty power raised Christ from the dead and seated Him in the place of honor at God's right hand in the heavenly realms. Now He is far above any ruler or authority or power or leader or anything else in this world or in the world to come. And God has put all things under the authority of Christ, and He gave Him this authority for the benefit of the Church. And the Church is His Body; it is filled by Christ, Who fills everything everywhere with His presence."[6.]

MAN IS FULFILLING PROPHECY

The Master's Plan gives many examples and illustrations showing the true state of man, his blindness, and inability to reason out the truth, truth of both the physical and the spiritual realms. Contrary to popular opinion, there is more to life than just physical existence. Captivated by a temporal worldview, many living comfortably in this present world would say, "I am rich, and increased with goods, and have need of nothing." The truth is, because God is eternal, His view of life is also eternal.

To the temporal minded, the rich of this world, He says, "But you do not realize that you are wretched, and miserable, and poor, and blind, and naked. I counsel you to buy from Me gold refined and tested by fire, so that you can become rich; and white clothes to wear, so that you can cover your shameful nakedness; and salve to put on your eyes, so that you can see."[7] We can account for the state of man when we understand that man born in sin; is born missing the mark. *In opening eyes, Jesus corrects our distorted view of life, thus giving man an opportunity to see a future in the Master's Plan.*

Man's spirit died in the Garden, God's Spiritual life left them after the fall.

While physically a man may think he is doing well, spiritually, he is dead and must be born again. When man sees life through the Spirit, he realizes the truth that he was, "Born wretched, but Jesus came to give him true joy.

— Born miserable, but Jesus gives peace. — Born poor, but Jesus gives him true riches. — *Born blind, but Jesus has opened his eyes.* — Born naked, but Jesus has covered all his sins."

In a late-night meeting with Jesus, Nicodemus, a great teacher in Israel, knew there had to be a greater power at work in the life of Jesus. Nicodemus knew Jesus could not be doing what they reported of Him unless God sent Him. Secretly, he went to see Jesus on a mission of discovery. However, before he could ask, Jesus answered, I assure you most solemnly I tell you, "unless one is born again (anew, from above), he cannot ever *see* the kingdom of God." Nicodemus then asked, "How can a man be born again when he is old? Can he enter his mother's womb again and be born?" Jesus answered, "I assure you most solemnly I tell you, unless one is born of water and even the Spirit, he cannot *enter* the Kingdom of God."

Man can only reproduce human life, but the Holy Spirit gives new life from heaven.[8] In Christ, God has given man a second chance, an opportunity to be born again. For although a person can read the Scriptures, they will not be able to understand them if they have not been born again, and *their eyes opened by the Holy Spirit.* Without His (the Spirits) help, they (the Scriptures) are foolish, and have little meaning, and this explains why so many do not understand what they are reading. However, these same Scriptures are food and nourishment to the spirit of the people of Faith. Listen, "If you are born twice, you will die once, maybe; if you are born once, you will die twice, and that's for certain." "Eternal Life is knowing God and knowing Jesus Christ, the One Whom He sent, this is Eternal Life." New Birth is where the Journey begins. If you do not know Him, "He now stands at your door, knocking."

> *The Preacher warns us to: "Remember your Creator earnestly now before the silver cord of life is snapped apart, or the golden bowl is broken, or the pitcher is broken at the fountain, or the wheel broken at the cistern and the whole circulatory system of the blood ceases to function; Then shall the dust out of which God made man's body return to the earth as it was, and the spirit shall return to God Who gave it. Vapor of vapors and futility of futilities, says the Preacher. All is futility (emptiness, falsity, vainglory, and transitoriness)!"[9]*

CHAPTER 14

Lord, Open our Eyes

The lamp of the body is the eye. Therefore, when your eye is good, your whole body also is full of light. But when your eye is bad, your body also is full of darkness.[1]

And beginning with Moses and all the Prophets, He explained to them what was said in all the Scriptures concerning Himself... Then their eyes were opened, and they recognized Him, and He disappeared from their sight... They asked each other, "Were not our hearts burning within us while He talked with us on the road and opened the Scriptures to us?"[2]

LET HIM OPEN YOUR EYES

The Road to Emmaus

Shortly after the death and resurrection of our Lord Jesus Christ, two of His followers were walking from Jerusalem to a village called Emmaus (about seven miles). They were talking with each other about everything that had happened. As they talked and discussed these things with each other, Jesus Himself came up and walked with them; but they were kept from recognizing Him. He asked them, "What are you discussing together as you walk along?" They stood still, their faces downcast. One of them, named Cleopas, asked Him, "Are you only a visitor to Jerusalem and do not know the things that have happened there in these days?" "What things?" He asked. "About Jesus of Nazareth," they replied. "He was a Prophet, powerful in word and deed before God and all the people. The chief priests and our rulers handed Him over to be sentenced to death, and they crucified Him; but we had hoped that He was the One Who was going to redeem Israel. And what is more, it is the third day since all this took place. In addition, some of our women amazed us. They went to the tomb early this morning but did not find His body. They came and told us they had seen a vision of angels, who said He was alive. Then some of our companions went to the tomb and found it just as the women had said, but Him they did not see." (See Luke 24:13-24).

Many of His followers who thought they understood the prophets stood baffled; they had not accepted Christ mission to come and die for the Sins of the entire world, although He had repeatedly told them. As was true of His many followers, these two on the road to Emmaus did not know the cross was the path to Glory.

But Christ rebuked them; He said to them, "How foolish you are, and how slow of heart to believe all that the prophets have spoken! Must not the Christ {Or Messiah} suffer these things and then enter His glory?" And beginning with Moses and all the Prophets, He explained to them what was said in all the Scriptures concerning Himself. As they approached the village to which they were going, Jesus acted as if He were going further. But they urged Him strongly, "Stay with us, for it is nearly evening; the day is almost over." So, He went in to stay with them. When He was at the table with them, He took bread, gave thanks, broke it, and began to give it to them.

THEN THEIR EYES OPENED AND THEY RECOGNIZED HIM, AND HE DISAPPEARED FROM THEIR SIGHT. (See Luke 24:25-31).

Now the Scripture says, "And beginning with Moses and all the Prophets, He explained to them what was said in all the Scriptures concerning Himself." We of course can only guess what the Master said to these disciples but let us do a brief review.

HIS MISSION

Thus, God sent His anointed Son into this world and resurrected Him after He died on the Cross. During His short ministry of a little over three years, He trained disciples and offered deliverance to those held captive and under the power of Satan, "the god of this world" (Age).

As the Lord and Savior of all those who have come to understand our need for Salvation. He came to die on a cross; He took our place and death sentence, and in so doing took away the sin of the world, thus fulfilling God's Promise to Eve in the Garden. God had said that of her seed (the Seed of the woman), One would come Who would bruise the head of the serpent. Satan is the one who continues to urge disobedience to the commands of

God. He was the instigator who caused mankind's fall, in the garden. In the Cross, Christ received a wound on His heel but dealt a crushing blow to Satan's head and, thus, his plan (although God has not carried out his sentence yet).

Before the Lord went to the Cross, in the wilderness He had to endure the test of obedience that Adam and Eve went through in the Garden. Through disobedience, the first parents of our race rebelled against the command of God, plunging the whole race into sin and death (separation from God). Because we, their posterity (humanity), were still within their loins (their genes, chromosomes, DNA), we through birth inherited the sinful nature, born subject to sin. Nevertheless, God's infinite love and mercy provided the means of restoring the fellowship broken by sin, thus putting man back on course through a Savior, God Himself making restitution for the breach that disobedience made. He did this by sending His Son in the likeness of sinful flesh, to redeem that which was lost. [3]

TEMPTATION BY SATAN

*N*ow Jesus may have gone on to explain His mission in more detail to these disciples. He may have told them of the wilderness test, with Satan given opportunity to tempt Him with the hope that if He, through sinning, failed the test, it would disqualify Him from completing His mission. (God tests, Satan tempts). If Christ had failed, all hope of redeeming humanity would forever be lost, and he (Satan) would have kept his position, holding dominion over the Earth, which he gained by default when Adam the first man sinned. Remember, in one of the temptations, while trying to entice Him, Satan offered Christ all the kingdoms of this temporal world. He said, all this authority I will give You and their glory; *for this has been delivered to me*, and I give it to whomever I wish. Therefore, if You will worship me, all will be yours. [4] To this offer, Christ replied, "Get behind Me, Satan! For it is written, *'You shall worship the Lord your God, and Him only you will serve.'*"

Now Jesus did not dispute Satan's claim of authority over the kingdoms of the world, for He knew of the dominion that Adam had lost in the fall. He also knew of Satan's titles of "god of this age" and "prince, or ruler of this world."

> "IT WAS HIS PASSING OF THE TEST THAT QUALIFIED HIM TO BECOME THE SAVIOR OF MANKIND."

What He did, however, was respond to the enemy with the Word of God, focusing his attention back to the Truth. For by obedience, He came to regain the kingdoms of this world, which in disobedience the first Adam lost. Thus, the present arrangement of things will all change during the Tribulation when the seventh Angels trumpet begins to sound. When the seventh angel blows his trumpet then, there will be loud voices shouting in heaven: saying, "The kingdoms of this World have become the kingdoms of our Lord and of His Christ, and He shall reign forever and ever!"[5] In Christ, we see the goal of the Master's Plan is the subject of our Salvation. It was through enduring 40 days and nights in the wilderness, tempted by the Devil, and tested by God, that Christ passed the test. The test consisted of overcoming "the lust of the flesh, the lust of the eyes, and the pride of life."[6] "It was His passing the test, which qualified Him to become the Savior of mankind." He overcame in the wilderness, where Adam and Eve failed in the garden. After the test, "Jesus returned in the power of the Spirit to Galilee, and news of Him went out through the entire region. He taught in their synagogues, being glorified by all."

THE MISSION STATEMENT

"So, He came to Nazareth, where He had been brought up. And as His custom was, He went into the synagogue on the Sabbath day and stood up to read. And He was handed the book of the prophet Isaiah. And when He had opened the book, He found the place where it was Written: "The Spirit of the Sovereign LORD is on Me, because the LORD has anointed Me to preach good news to the poor. He has sent Me to bind up the brokenhearted, to proclaim freedom for the captives and release from darkness for the prisoners, to proclaim the year of the LORD's favor." And He closed the book, and He gave it back to the attendant and sat down. And the eyes of all who were in the synagogue were fixed on Him. And He began to say to them, "Today this Scripture is fulfilled in your hearing." [7]

Isaiah lived from 740-680 B.C. In the book of Isaiah, Chapter 61:1-3, there is a clear reference to a twofold prophecy, which the Messiah (The Christ; the Anointed One) would fulfill. The Prophet writing some 700 years before the birth of Jesus Christ wrote saying, "The Spirit of the Sovereign LORD is on Me, because the LORD has anointed Me to preach good news to the poor. He has sent Me to bind up the brokenhearted, to proclaim freedom for the captives, and release from darkness for the prisoners, to proclaim the year of the LORD's favor." Isaiah 61:1, 2a. As you can see this is what Jesus read, when he stood up to read in the synagogue.

136

HE CAME TO SET THE CAPTIVES FREE

Jesus accepted His calling, having publicly declared that it was He Who had come to fulfill the Prophecies, thus we see the fulfillment in Luke's Gospel (4:18, 19), which says of Jesus, God anointed and sent Him:

1. To preach the gospel to the poor
2. To heal the brokenhearted
3. To proclaim liberty to the captives
4. To bring recovery of sight to the blind
5. To set at liberty the oppressed
6. To proclaim the acceptable year of the LORD

Fulfilling Prophecy, Jesus did everything wonderfully. Fulfilling His mission, He said, "Only the sick need a Doctor."

PROPHECY: CHRIST'S MISSION, GOD SENT HIM

God anointed His Son to preach the Good News to the poor. Through the Spirit, God anointed Jesus to preach the Gospel, "the Good News." He fulfilled the Promise made to Eve in the Garden; the Promised Seed had come. "His Anointing was a baptism in the Power of the Holy Ghost to go forth and boldly preach the Gospel." "Repent, the Kingdom of God is at hand, for the Lamb of God has come." This is the "Good News;" God was healing the breach in the Kingdom, providing forgiveness of sin, and restoring fellowship with man. Through the Spirit, God led Him to the poor; those whom God foreknew would receive the "Good News" with joy.

God sent His Son to heal the brokenhearted. The Gospels reveal many occasions in which He healed people. God wants us to be whole. With power, God sent Him to heal those who, because of their plight in life, were heartbroken, grief-stricken, and miserable, yet kept a confident hope in God. The Hope of Jesus has healed many a broken and wounded heart. God fixes broken people; He heals broken hearts and then uses them to reach others. In one instance, He was summoned to the house of a ruler, whose daughter was dying, "As Jesus went with him, He was surrounded by the crowds. And there was a woman in the crowd who had had a hemorrhage for twelve years. She had spent everything she had on doctors and still could find no cure. She came up behind Jesus and *touched the fringe of His robe. Immediately, the bleeding stopped.*

"'Who touched Me?' Jesus asked.

"Everyone denied it, and Peter said, 'Master, this whole crowd is pressing up against you.' But Jesus told him, *'No, someone deliberately touched Me, for I felt healing power go out from Me.'* When the woman realized that Jesus knew, *she began to tremble and fell to her knees before Him.* The whole crowd heard her explain why she had touched Him and that she had been at once healed. 'Daughter,' He said to her, *'your faith has made you whole. Go in peace.'"*[8]

God sent His Son to proclaim liberty to the captives. The time had come to release the prisoners bound in Satan's P.O.W. camps of this world. Slaves held by a temporal-mind-set, in the strongholds of wickedness, the power grips of sins bondage, and the constant fear of death. God wants us free in our minds. By grace, through faith God set us free, free to follow an eternal mind-set, the mind of Christ. Christ's teachings proclaimed our liberty, as explained by such phrases as, "Will you be made whole?" And "your sins are forgiven, Go in Peace."

God sent His Son to bring recovery of sight to the blind. The Gospels abound with examples of His restoring sight (physical and spiritual). In doing so, He fulfilled this, and many other prophecies found in the book of Isaiah. He did this, *"To open eyes that are blind,* to free captives from prison, and to release from the dungeon those who sit in darkness."[9] Again, Isaiah said, "In that day the deaf will hear the words of the scroll, and out of gloom and darkness the eyes of the blind will see."[10] "Then will the eyes of the blind be *opened* and the ears of the deaf unstopped."[11]

God sent His Son to set at liberty the oppressed; He cast demons out of those oppressed of the Devil. After casting the "Legion" out of a demon-possessed man, the man sat at Jesus' feet clothed and in his right mind. When Jesus got back into the boat, the man who had been demon possessed begged to go, too. But Jesus said, "No, go home to your friends, and tell them what wonderful things the Lord has done for you and how merciful He has been." So, the man started off to visit the Ten Towns of that region and began to tell everyone about the wonderful things Jesus had done for him; and everyone was amazed at what he told them.[12]

God sent His Son to proclaim the acceptable year of the LORD. His Ministry began with John the Baptist proclaiming to the people, "Repent, for the Kingdom of God is at hand."

However, later after Herod cast John the Baptist into prison, he began to doubt whether Jesus was in fact "the Messiah." John sent two of his disciples who said to Him, "Are You the Coming One, or do we look for another?" Jesus answered and said to them, "Go and tell John the things which you hear and see: 'The blind receive sight, the lame walk, those who have leprosy are cured, the deaf hear, the dead are raised, and the good news is preached to the poor.'"[13] This was all a direct confirmation of Isaiah's Prophecy. Remember, before His birth, the angel said to Joseph, "She (Mary) will bring forth a Son, and you shall call His name JESUS, for He will save His people from their sins." This was the babe whose birth, an angel announced to shepherds in the field. The same babe we picture as, "the One in the manger." Even now two thousand years later, we still celebrate His birth at Christmas, and His resurrection on Easter.

About Christ's fulfillment of Prophecies, when we look back over the Old Testament, we see that as the Son of Man, He fulfilled many prophecies during His first coming. "For the blind received their sight, the lame walked, those who had leprosy and various other diseases and ailments, He cured, the deaf heard, He raised the dead to life and preached the good news to the poor." However, we quickly realize that far too many other prophecies saw fulfillment for this to be coincidence, and yet the truth gets more exciting, when we see all the unfulfilled prophecies, demanding a "Second Coming." In the Synagogue when Jesus stood up to read, He stopped reading right in the middle of Isaiah's prophecy. Here we see the events of the first and second comings separated only by a comma. The second half of what the Prophet wrote Christ will fulfill at His Second Coming. *The part, which He did not read, says this,* "And the day of vengeance of our God, to comfort all who mourn, and provide for those who grieve in Zion—to bestow on them a crown of beauty instead of ashes, the oil of gladness instead of mourning, and a garment of praise instead of a spirit of despair. They will be called oaks of righteousness, a planting of the LORD for the display of His splendor." (Isaiah 61:2b, 3). Having arisen from the dead, and ascended into Heaven, we know that He will one day return, to fulfill the last half. He will return in the time of "Jacob's Trouble," when the nation and people of Israel will have come through a severe time of testing, trial, and suffering during the "Great Tribulation." Then the nation and those who have survived the devastation and destruction will be in such a state, to allow perfect fulfillment of this prophecy. [14] Then with great mourning, they will look upon the One Whom they pierced.[15]

This whole topic could easily provide us with subject matter for another book.

THAT BURNING IN THE HEART KIND OF TRUTH

But, let us pick up where we left off with the disciples walking with Jesus on the road to Emmaus, the two with whom He sat at the table took bread, blessed and broke it, and gave it to them, and afterwards vanished from their sight. After which, they asked each other, "Were not our hearts burning within us while He talked with us on the road and *opened the Scriptures to us?*" They got up and returned at once to Jerusalem. There they found the eleven and those with them assembled and saying, "It is true! The Lord has risen and has appeared to Simon." Then the two told what had happened on the road, and how they recognized Jesus when He broke the bread.

Jesus appears to the Disciples

While they were still talking about this, Jesus Himself stood among them and said to them, "Peace be with you." They were startled and frightened, thinking they saw a ghost (spirit). He said to them, "Why are you troubled, and why do doubts rise in your minds (hearts)? Look at My hands and My feet. It is I Myself! "Touch Me and see; *a ghost (spirit) does not have flesh and bones, as you see I have.*" When He had said this, He showed them His hands and feet. And while they still did not believe it because of joy and amazement, He asked them, "Do you have anything here to eat?" They gave Him a piece of broiled fish, and some honeycomb, and He took *it* and ate it in their presence.

The Scriptures Opened

He said to them, "This is what I told you while I was still with you: Everything must be fulfilled that is written about Me in the Law of Moses the Prophets and the Psalms." *Then He opened their minds* so they could understand the Scriptures. He said, "This is what is written: The Christ {The Messiah} will suffer and rise from the dead on the third day, and repentance and forgiveness of sins will be preached in His Name to all nations, beginning at Jerusalem. You are witnesses of these things. I Am going to send you what My Father has promised; but stay in the city until you have been clothed with power from on high." (See Luke 24:32-49).

> *It is because of the witness and testimony of many over the years that "we know that the Son of God has come and has given us understanding, that we may know Him Who is true; and we are in Him Who is true, in His Son Jesus Christ. This is the true God and Eternal Life."* [16]

PHYSICAL BIRTH – AND THE MIRACLE OF PHYSICAL EYESIGHT

The Blind Man who saw

Now as He went along, He saw a man blind from birth. His disciples asked Him, "Rabbi, who sinned, this man or his parents, that he was born blind?" "Neither this man nor his parents sinned," said Jesus, *"but this happened so that the work of God might be displayed in his life.* As long as it is day, we must do the work of Him Who sent Me. Night is coming, when no one can work.

While I AM in the World, I AM the Light of the World."

Having said this, he spat on the ground, made some mud with the saliva, and put it on the man's eyes. "Go," He told him, "wash in the Pool of Siloam" (this word means Sent). So the man went and washed and came home seeing. His neighbors and those who had formerly seen him begging asked, "Isn't this the same man who used to sit and beg?" Some claimed that he was. Others said, "No, he only looks like him." But he himself insisted, "I am the man." *"How then were your eyes opened?"* They demanded. He replied, "The man they call Jesus made some mud and put it on my eyes. He told me to go to Siloam and wash. So, I went and washed, and then I could see." "Where is this man?" They asked him. "I don't know," he said. They brought to the Pharisees the man who had been blind.

Now the day on which Jesus had made the mud and *opened the man's eyes* was a Sabbath. Therefore, the Pharisees also asked him how he had received his sight. "He put mud on my eyes," the man replied, "and I washed, and now I see." Some of the Pharisees said, "This man is not from God, for he does not keep the Sabbath." But others asked, "How can a sinner do such miraculous signs?" So they were divided. Finally, they turned again to the blind man, "What have you to say about him? *It was your eyes he opened.*" The man replied, "He is a prophet."

The Jews still *did not believe* that he had been blind and had received his sight until they sent for the man's parents. "Is this your son?" They asked. "Is this the one you say was born blind? How is it that now he can see?" "We know he is our son," the parents answered, "and we know he was born blind. But how he can see now, or *who opened his eyes,* we do not know. Ask him. He is of age; he will speak for himself." His parents said this because they were afraid of the Jews, for already the Jews had decided that anyone who acknowledged that Jesus was the Christ {Or Messiah} would be put out of the synagogue. That was why his parents said, "He is of age; ask him." A second time they summoned the man who had been blind. "Give glory to God," {A solemn charge to tell the truth–Joshua 7:19} they said. "We know this man is a sinner." He replied, "Whether he is a sinner or not, I do not know. *ONE THING I DO KNOW. I WAS BLIND BUT NOW I SEE!"*

Then they asked him, "What did He do to you? *How did He open your eyes?"* He answered, "I have told you already and you did not listen. Why do you want to hear it again? Do you want to become His disciples, too?" Then they hurled insults at him and said, *"You are this fellow's disciple! We are disciples of Moses!* We know that God spoke to Moses, but as for this fellow, we do not even know where He comes from." The man answered, "Now that is remarkable! You do not know where He comes from, yet *He opened my eyes.* We know that God does not listen to sinners. He listens to the godly man who does His will. *Nobody has ever heard of opening the eyes of a man born blind.* If this man were not from God, He could do nothing." To this they replied, "You were steeped in sin at birth; how dare you lecture us!" And they threw him out.

Jesus heard that they had thrown him out, and when He found him, He said, *"Do you believe in the Son of Man?"* "Who is he, sir?" The man asked. "Tell me so that I may believe in Him." Jesus said, "You have now seen Him; in fact, He is the One speaking with you." Then the man said, *"Lord, I believe,"* and he worshipped Him. Jesus said, *"For judgment I have come into this world, so that the blind will see and those who see will become blind."* Some Pharisees, who were with him, heard him say this and asked, "What? Are we blind too?" Jesus said, "If you were blind, you would not be guilty of sin; but now that you claim you can see, your guilt stays. [17]

SPIRITUAL (NEW) BIRTH – AND
THE MIRACLE OF SPIRITUAL EYESIGHT
Saul: A Man made blind so that he could see

Meanwhile, Saul was still breathing out murderous threats against the Lord's disciples. He went to the high priest and asked him for letters to the synagogues in Damascus, so if he found any there who belonged to the Way, whether men or women, he might take them as prisoners to Jerusalem. As he neared Damascus on his journey, suddenly a light from heaven flashed around him.

He fell to the ground and heard a voice say to him, "SAUL, SAUL, WHY DO YOU PERSECUTE ME?" "Who are you, Lord?" Saul asked. "I AM JESUS, WHOM YOU ARE PERSECUTING," He replied. "Now get up and go into the city, and you will be told what you must do." The men traveling with Saul stood there speechless; they heard the sound but did not see anyone.

SAUL GOT UP FROM THE GROUND, BUT WHEN HE OPENED HIS EYES, HE COULD SEE NOTHING. So they led him by the hand into Damascus. For three days he was blind, and did not eat or drink anything. In Damascus there was a disciple named Ananias. The Lord called to him in a vision, "Ananias!" "Yes, Lord," he answered. The Lord told him, "Go to the house of Judas on Straight Street and ask for a man from Tarsus named Saul, for he is praying. In a vision he has seen a man named Ananias come and place his hands on him to restore his sight." "Lord," Ananias answered, "I have heard many reports about this man and all the harm he has done to Your saints in Jerusalem. And he has come here with authority from the chief priests to arrest all who call on Your name."

But the Lord said to Ananias, "Go! This man is My chosen instrument to carry My name before the Gentiles and their kings and before the people of Israel. I will show him how much he must suffer for My name." Then Ananias went to the house and entered it. Placing his hands on Saul, he said, "Brother Saul, the Lord—Jesus, Who appeared to you on the road as you were coming here—has sent me so that you may see again and be filled with the Holy Spirit." Immediately, something like scales fell from Saul's eyes, and he could see again. He got up and was baptized, and after taking some food, he regained his strength. Saul spent several days with the disciples in Damascus. At once, he began to preach in the synagogues that Jesus is the Son of God. All those who heard him were astonished and asked, "Isn't he the man who caused havoc in Jerusalem among those who call on this name? And hasn't he come here to take them as prisoners to the chief priests?" Yet Saul grew increasingly powerful and baffled the Jews living in Damascus by proving that Jesus is the Christ. (Or Messiah)[18]

> THIS MAN IS MY CHOSEN INSTRUMENT TO CARRY MY NAME BEFORE THE GENTILES AND THEIR KINGS AND BEFORE THE PEOPLE OF ISRAEL.

Saul (Paul)[19] repeated his testimony again in Acts 22:6-16, *before the people of Israel* and in Acts 26:12-18, *before a king*, lastly, he went *before the Caesar at Rome*. Before them, He recounted his conversion and how he at first eagerly persecuted the early Church, as a Pharisee he received authority from the chief priests. He had many believers shut up in prison, and was in full agreement giving his vote, when those who called upon the Name of Jesus were put to death. He went on to say, "While thus occupied, as

I journeyed to Damascus with authority and commission from the chief priests, at midday, O king, along the road I saw a light from heaven, brighter than the sun, shining around me and those who journeyed with me. And when we all had fallen to the ground, I heard a voice speaking to me and saying in the Hebrew language, 'Saul, Saul, why are you persecuting Me? It is hard for you to kick against the goads.' So, I said, 'Who are You, Lord?' And He said, 'I Am Jesus, whom you are persecuting. But rise and stand on your feet; for I have appeared to you for this purpose, to make you a minister and a witness both the things which you have seen and of the things which I will yet reveal to you. *I will deliver you from the Jewish people, as well as from the Gentiles, to whom I now send you, to open their eyes, in order to turn them from darkness to light, and from the power of Satan to God, that they may receive forgiveness of sins and an inheritance among those who are sanctified by faith in Me.'"*[20]

The miracle that Paul gained was direct access to revelations from the Lord. Through revelations, the Lord gave him great wisdom and insight into the Masters Plan and Purposes for the Church. His ministry was to feed the Gentile (spiritual) offspring of Abraham. Much of what Paul learned he gave to us in his inspired letters written to the Churches, which he had helped to found and begin. His letters, written to the early Church, hold timeless spiritual truths, as refreshing today as the day the Holy Spirit inspired him to write them. God preserved them for us.

Outside the Gospels, his 14 Letters form a major part of the New Testament. Now Paul wrote the following Church Letters: Romans to the Church in Rome. First and second Corinthians to the Church in Corinth. Galatians to the Church in Galatia. Ephesians to the Church in Ephesus. Philippians to the Church in Philippi. Colossians to the Church in Colosse. First and second Thessalonians to the Church in Thessalonica. And more likely than not the book of Hebrews to the Jews scattered abroad. He also wrote Letters to three of his disciples, "sons in the Faith." To Philemon the letter of Philemon, to Timothy the letters of first and second Timothy and to Titus the letter of Titus.

Thus, in Paul, God had a chosen vessel, appointed to share the Good News of God's grace, and give us greater insight into the Master's Plan. The Lord Jesus Christ inspired the visions and revelations in his writings, as he recounts in the following: "For indeed I did not receive it from man, nor was I taught it, but *it came to me* through a *direct* revelation *given* by Jesus Christ (the Messiah). You have heard of my earlier career and former manner of life in the Jewish religion (Judaism), how I persecuted and abused the Church of God furiously and extensively, and *with fanatical zeal did my best* to make havoc of it and destroy it. And *you have heard how* I outstripped many of the men of my own generation among the people of my race in *my advancement in study and observance of the laws of* Judaism, so extremely enthusiastic and zealous I was for the traditions of my ancestors.

But when He, Who had chosen and set me apart even before I was born and had called me by His grace (His undeserved favor and blessing), saw fit and was pleased to reveal (unveil, disclose) His Son within me so that I might proclaim Him among the Gentiles (the non-Jewish world) as the glad tidings (Gospel), immediately I did not confer with flesh and blood *did not consult or counsel with any frail human being or communicate with anyone.*" [21]

But God speaks again and again, though people do not recognize it. He speaks in dreams, in visions of the night when deep sleep falls on people as they lie in bed. He whispers in their ear and terrifies them with His warning. He causes them to change their minds; He keeps them from pride. He keeps them from the grave, from crossing over the river of death. Or God disciplines people with sickness and pain, with ceaseless aching in their bones. They lose their appetite and do not care for even the most delicious food. They waste away to skin and bones. They are at death's door; the angels of death wait for them. "But if a special messenger from heaven is there to intercede for a person, to declare that he is upright, God will be gracious and say, 'Set him free. Do not make him die, for I have found a ransom for his life.' Then his body will become as healthy as a child's, firm and youthful again. When he prays to God, he will be accepted. And God will receive him with joy and restore him to good standing. He will declare to his friends, 'I sinned, but it was not worth it. God rescued me from the grave, and now my life is filled with light.'" Yes, God often does these things for people. He rescues them from the grave so they may live in the light of the living.22

Part 6 –

Intelligent Designs

CHAPTER 15

Intelligent Designs

The Prophet Jeremiah wrote, "Ah, Sovereign LORD, You have made the heavens and the earth by Your great power and outstretched arm. Nothing is too hard for You."1

THE DESIGNER CREATOR

Creation reveals the work of the three people of the Godhead. We see the hand of the Designer Creator revealed all around us. His Word gives much insight into the nature of Creation, spiritual, and material.

Wherever you look; seeing the beauty and intricacies of Creation, you see the hand of the Creator. Whether in varieties and types or patterns and hues they all unveil His design, whether on land, in the seas or in the heavens. Look at your fingerprints, a seashell, or a snowflake; they are all wonders of His Creation. Whether flowers, their beauty and fragrance, or a simple blade of grass, the oceans, the mountains or the stars, or the many varieties in types of bird, fish, animal, and insect life, each with their own complexity and uniqueness.

Each has a role, each design has a set specific purpose. Take a microscope, look, and see. Look at the marvel of your own body and its inner workings with all its networking parts: your fingers, arms or legs, your eyes, and ears. Each one performs a specific role given to them by design, each one designed to serve. And yet there is beauty, you can see this in plants, animals, and all of Creation. Besides beauty, there is harmony; for example, consider your internal organs serving individual roles and purposes, they all work together to support and preserve you. Look at your mouth and nose, your heart, and lungs or even your brain; they all serve a unique purpose by design. They all work with the atmosphere, the air, the water, and the earth itself. Your body takes food and water out of the environment from which it came. Look all around you and see the work of the hands of the Creator. The sheer volume of what exists in the natural world around us is staggering. There is order in the world, the sun and moon, the stars, galaxies, all serving a purpose, each having a role by design. "And yet,

MEN HAVE SUPPRESSED THE TRUTH."

Anyone with his or her *eyes opened* can see that with all this order, Creation has all the marks of existing according to a prearranged plan and purpose. Life is moving toward a predetermined purpose or end, and all of it points to an "Intelligent Design." However, it is not the evidence, but your worldview that controls what you see. Through science, and his God given senses of sight, sound, taste, touch, and smell, man has developed many tools as he tries to understand the works of God in the world around him and his environment. God placed "man" at the top of His Creation. By an act of his will (worldview), man can choose to either see the balance and harmony of this design or ignore the evidence seeing it all as a great accident of random chance.

Man through observation, by experimentation, by measuring and recording has sought to prove the laws that govern God's work in and of Creation. But recently, science has undergone a startling evolution, once a tool that man used to study and understand the many works of God, it has now become the determinate of whether He even exist.

It is not by accident the Scripture says, "the fool says in his heart, 'There is no God.'"[2] Neither accident nor random chance could ever create the laws that we see in Creation. In this world of social progress (social politics), Believers in the fields of cosmology and biology who speak out against the travesty men are perpetrating against society do so realizing that they may be committing professional suicide. Therefore, in our own days, the leaders of science as in many other disciplines are to often the leaders of infidelity. It seems that without special grace, man is incapable of bearing the slightest weight of power on his shoulders, without losing his balance, as he tries in vain to glorify himself.

Thus, the Scriptures take just the attitude we should expect. They altogether avoid contact with the science of men, "For God's holy wrath and indignation are revealed from heaven against all ungodliness and unrighteousness of men, who *in their wickedness repress and hinder the truth* and make it inoperative. For what can be known about God is clear to them and made plain in their inner consciousness, because God *Himself* has shown it to them. For since the Creation of the WORLD God's invisible qualities—His Eternal Power and Divine Nature—have been clearly seen, being understood from what has been made, so that men are without excuse."[3] Now, God does not forbid us to search as far as we can into the laws of His universe; but He refuses to aid our studies by revelation. For the present, He would rather have us attentive to our spiritual and thus moral transformation and that of our fellow-creatures. However, after a short season He will open immeasurable stores of His riches in wisdom and knowledge to those who love and trust Him and delight their souls to see the secrets of His creative power.

It is a temporal worldview that causes men of Science, Politics, and Law to betray the trust given them, when they do not uphold the principles of truth, honesty, and integrity. They trade principles for purposes of amassing wealth (greed), power (every impurity and sexual immorality), acceptance and or personal recognition. They sacrifice eternal truth for temporal pleasures. All around us, the whole universe shouts "Intelligent Design." Unlike frail man, there is something about the stars, which speak of intransience (eternalness).

During the many generations that have come and gone on earth, despite evil, the Creator is still fulfilling His purpose and work as He keeps and preserves countless life forms, each one revealing both His wisdom and Intelligent Design. To suggest that Christ, and not some accident, is the source of Creation is a strange idea to most people. *You can only see this if your heart and mind are open,* and you have not fallen for *"The Lie."* Some claim a secret knowledge of the truth, apart from Christ. These are simply liars and children of the Devil. As we have come to expect, this is the same group promoting the "nothing times nothing, equals all scandal."

Truth is, "life can only come from life," all life is dependent on other life. The lower on the higher; the simple on the complex; the powerless on the powerful; the impersonal on the personal; the unintelligent on the intelligent; the nonexistent on the existing; the natural on the spiritual; the temporary on the eternal. "Nothing can come from nothing or be produced by nothing." How bold is the lie of the evolutionist, who says that everything came from nothing. By comparison, the theory of evolution is the equivalent of saying that a tornado rolled through a junkyard and produced a Laptop computer. It boggles the mind that someone would believe and then try to convince others to believe and fall for the same old lie. It seems the bigger the lie the easier it is to swallow its all-absurd.

It should be obvious to all of us that "there are no self-initiating developments. Someone created the Laptop computer, someone created man and the rest of creation. Now the word evolution means progress. We know that every event, every development has a cause. This is the law of "Cause and Effect," which is the same as the principle of "sowing and reaping" found in the Word. The argument of "Creation versus Evolution" is deceptive at best. For while evolution looks at the progress of the event, creation speaks of a Creator, "a cause" for the event. God was the cause; creation was the effect or event. Only the deceived would fall for the lies and deceptions needed to support what men have imagined and called "evolution." Like so many other lies poured out on society today, it is evil and deceptive what those who willfully promote this lie do, thus confirming since the fall, that humankind consists of two kinds of seeds, one fundamentally good, and the other evil.

Surely, in vain the net is spread in the sight of any bird,[4]

The Fool has said in his heart, "There is no God."

When you look at the rate and increase in knowledge, when you consider the inroads made in various disciplines, which study the human body, or the evidence found in hormones, and genetic research into DNA, or even the science of "Nano-technology." For instance, research into this science reveals design and order in creation on a unimaginable scale only a few years ago. This science is looking into ways of manipulating the building blocks of material Creation. Yet in fact, what is more remarkable is that no intelligent person would look at a work of man and presume to say; "It developed all by itself," without any external influence; "how absurd." Yet, none of us has heard a peep from men who are now seeing the miraculous and the many wonders found in the micro miniature world all around us. Nevertheless, what would happen if a student dared to take a stand in a biology class saying, "I don't believe in the theory of evolution, there's just too much *open and visible evidence* supporting Intelligent Design and a

> I DON'T BELIEVE IN THE THEORY OF EVOLUTION; THERE'S JUST TOO MUCH OPEN AND VISIBLE EVIDENCE SUPPORTING INTELLIGENT DESIGN AND A CREATOR.

Creator." This student would face a battery of peer-inflicted censorship, criticism, and rebuke, scoffed at, and held up to high ridicule, their motives disparaged, and sanity questioned; again, "How absurd is this." And you can expect the same response if the subject were Abortion, Gay Marriage, or any other travesty of depravity, promoted by those in darkness. Yet, an intellectually honest and *open-minded* person evaluating and weighing the evidence would at once see a flaw in the views and values of the many so-called experts. The message here is that "Truth is an acceptable sacrifice on the altar of good intentions." The good intentions here are, "We don't want to offend people who might hold a different view of the truth."

This Biblically predicted state of men ought to tell you something. Paul wrote, "But God's angry displeasure erupts as acts of human mistrust and wrongdoing and lying accumulate, as people try to put a shroud over Truth. Nevertheless, the basic reality of God is plain enough. *Open your eyes and there it is!* By taking a long and thoughtful look at what God has created, people have always been able to see what their eyes as such cannot see: Eternal Power, for instance, and the mystery of His divine being. Therefore, nobody has a good excuse.

What happened was this: People knew God perfectly well, but when they did not treat Him like God, refusing to worship Him, they trivialized themselves into silliness and confusion so that there was neither sense nor direction left in their lives. They pretended to know it all but were illiterate about life. They traded the glory of God who holds the entire world in His hands for cheap figurines you can buy at any roadside stand.

Therefore, God said, in effect, "If that's what you want, that's what you get." It was not long before they were living in a pig-pen, smeared with filth, filthy inside and out. In addition, all this because they traded the true God for a fake god and worshipped the god they made instead of the God Who made them—the God we bless, the God Who blesses us.

Oh, yes! Worse followed. Refusing to know God, they soon did not know how to be human either—women did not know how to be women, men did not know how to be men. Sexually confused, they abused and defiled one another, women with women, men with men—all lust, no love. Then they paid for it, oh, how they paid for it—emptied of God and love, godless and loveless wretches. Since they did not bother to acknowledge God, God quit bothering them and let them run loose.

Then all hell broke loose: Rampant evil, grabbing and grasping, vicious backstabbing. They made life hell on earth with their envy, wanton killing, bickering, and cheating. Look at them: Mean-spirited, venomous, fork-tongued God-bashers. Bullies, swaggerers, insufferable windbags! They keep inventing new ways of wrecking lives. They ditch their parents when they get in the way. Stupid, slimy, cruel, cold-blooded. Moreover, it is not as if they do not know better. They know perfectly well they are spitting in God's face. Moreover, they do not care—worse, they hand out prizes to those who do the worst things best![5]

Secularists, who in their worldview consider truth irrelevant, and hatred or denial of the existence of God normal, not only support, but they also encourage these behaviors. Is it any wonder that in the last few generations people have sought numerous ways to rid society of common sense, the stigma of guilt, and the shame connected with sin? Today many well-intentioned but deceived people stand confused, without a sense of purpose or direction in life. Is it any wonder, since many through conditioning have unsuspectingly bought into an "acceptance mind-set," which says, there is no God, there are no moral absolutes, everything is relative, and "anything goes." Many in leadership and authority have rejected the standard of Truth, not realizing in doing so, that they embrace a Lie. When truth is without God, all they have is a puzzle, a puzzle with many missing pieces, an incomplete picture, yet they insist the rest of us share their vision, for only they have the intelligence to see the complete picture. Yet when you look at the proof, why should anyone give in to such nonsense, it is irrational. Excuse me if this offends your sensitivity, but our goal here is to get you to see the truth.

"Can you see the need for a Wake-Up call,
Can you see a need for Revival!"

Listen, you do not have to be anybody's fool. The only evolution that a man can hope to experience is a transformation and resurrection into a new creation. While we have all had exposure, how much of "the Lie" have you believed? About this crowd, God said, "While they claimed to be wise, they became fools." What they do not know is, "God is watching; He sees men's actions and choices," while no one, by choice needs believe, no one needs to die and go to hell either. Listen, the world does not love you; the world is not your friend. If the people who belong to this world will lie to you, and tell you, it is the truth, that is not love. The temporal mind-set dominating this world is the product of a satanic stronghold; it is from this stronghold that Christ came, to set us free.

The Scripture says, "Woe to those who call evil good, and good evil; Who put darkness for light, and light for darkness; Who put bitter for sweet, and sweet for bitter!"⁶

Those who keep men in darkness are not doing them any favors. This life on earth is not, "all about you." It is about the Cross and what He did! It is about God's love and His Plan for you. Despite all the evidence, still "The fool says in his heart, "There is no God." It is a shame; even the conditioning that little children must go through. The dirty little secret is this, "If the haters of truth were to admit the God of the Bible as the source of all Creation; they would have to admit many other things too."

Look and See, "The Fingerprints of God"

God's fingerprints are all over Creation, look around and you see His variety everywhere, everything that man might make, no matter what it is, God made the materials. He created atoms, molecules, genes, chromosomes, and cells. He made them similar and different; He made each one unique. You are unique; we are all unique, there never has been, nor will there ever be, another you. Look at your hands and see your fingertips, your fingerprints; your eyes are unique, they identify you. The Truth is this; you and I are special creations. God created DNA as "the Master Plan for all physical life, plant, and animal." God programmed our DNA at conception. He created every part, and all our distinct features; none of this is the product of blind chance, or an accident; it is the work of a loving Father and Creator. He purposely programmed our DNA and thus our physical body to be exactly who we are. In Chapter 12— "A Book in Heaven"—we read in Psalms 139, that the Creator had

> GOD CREATED DNA AS "THE MASTER PLAN FOR ALL PHYSICAL LIFE, PLANT, AND ANIMAL."

knowledge of us, even before we existed in the womb. Mentally and emotionally, we were all born with a clean slate; our temperament, life experiences, and our responses to those life experiences became the clay, shaping our character and personality, thus forming the person that we have become. God, by design, prescribed this order for our growth and development. We carry (the inner person) the fruit, who we are, whether good or bad, with us into the next life. God does not play games; He is the Giver of Laws, and a God of Order.

Personal choices take on greater significance when we, as Believers, realize we can become stronger in our walk of faith, by choice, just as we become who we are, by choice. This is why God is so concerned about fruit; those who align with His Laws align with His Will; to have things arranged any other way would be a distortion. He gave us Commands and Laws to govern our behavior, Laws that if we follow yield the blessings that He promised to those who love and obey Him. His Promise was Eternal Life. God tests His creatures; He looks for those who will seek Him out and obey His Will. Nevertheless, even suggesting that His reason for giving us Life has nothing to do with our knowing Him and His Word in this Life is foolish. If people do not accept Him in this life, how is it that He will accept them in the next? Will they be able to say, *"I didn't know or, it was a mistake?"*

> *"The eyes of the Lord are in everyplace,*
> *keeping watch upon the evil and the good."7*

Intelligent Designs—A Foundation for Faith

Science is in a quagmire, while there are many things that men of science know and can explain, there are still many more, the answers to which they do not have a clue.

The bumblebee happens to be one of them; theoretically Bumblebee's are not supposed to fly, but you cannot convince them, they keep right on flying anyway. Science has still not crossed the boundary of seeing the invisible; they assume invisible or spiritual matter does not exist. Stop and think if we can see His handiwork all around us in Creation, does it not make sense to get to know Him better through His Word. Now if according to the evolutionist argument, man is a being, evolved through evolution the question becomes, is he still evolving, and if so, into what." Besides, where is the proof? Rooted in many who reject God's Plan is a conviction of sin, guilt and a deep-seated self-loathing and hatred of the Truth.

Yet there are so many questions the theory of evolution cannot begin to answer, if you did not already know, you would wonder how men came to accept it. If you chose to inquire, you might ask questions like, "How did man become male and female?" "Why did they become male and female?" How was it possible for all species throughout the spectrums: birds, insects, mammals, and fish, to become male and female? *There are millions of animal species.* Being in separate bodies, which of the two changed first? How did they know of their need to come together? How did they find one another?

How did their sexual reproductive parts, which share a common design in many species throughout Creation, come into being? Why did they devise reproductive systems, what unique conditions caused this? Since reproduction is a prior condition to evolution, it cannot be a product of it. Therefore, we face the logical need for the original Creation of life and its power of continued reproduction. The power of reproduction is not in the embryo, but only in the mature parent. Was the first bird an egg, or a fully mature adult? An egg cannot produce an egg. It is also true the egg is not improvable by itself. Improvement can come only in and through the mature form. There must be a parent-form to produce an egg from which offspring can come. If evolution happened once, what stopped it, and will it happen again? It is becoming more obvious that this world is a battlefield in which truth and lies are the opponents and the souls of men the spoils. You can find Truth in short explanations; it is the lies that people stretch, because you must produce new ones to cover the old, while trying to keep some since of credibility. Nevertheless, the goal of the

> IT'S BECOMING MORE AND MORE OBVIOUS THAT THIS WORLD IS A BATTLEFIELD IN WHICH, TRUTH AND LIES ARE THE OPPONENTS AND THE SOULS OF MEN THE SPOILS.

temporal view is expediency, not consistency. If science supported evolution, there would be mountains of proof, "where's the mountain?" Neither evolutionists nor their theory will ever be able to explain the question of man's origin, *they cannot*. You cannot arrive at the truth through a set of false assumptions; you simply stumble, and falter past it.

Evolution is darkness, like Satan it opposes all truth, and rejects all light, especially the light of God's Word. Have you ever wondered why secular evolutionists rigidly oppose teaching the alternative, Creation, and Intelligent Design in the public arena? God forbid that anyone of those "young minds full of mush" should stumble onto the truth. Could it be that rebellion, hatred and hard-heartedness will not let some men believe anything but "The Lie." The Word says, "The fear of the LORD is the beginning of knowledge, but fools despise wisdom and discipline."[8] (The Hebrew word for "fool" means one who is morally deficient).

By default, they reveal the seed of the serpent within. Having rejected the Truth, and embraced a Lie, Satan has provided them with, "a theory of convenience," intended to allow those who should have known better, a means to ease a troubled conscience and continue in their sin. Do not they know that after their life here there will be an accounting, a judgment, where the souls of men will see either glory or damnation.

"Men will have to give their account to God, not the Devil."

Although you will not see it on the evening news or the front-page headlines, for some time now, scientists have been proving that Intelligent Design, and not blind chance, is the cause behind Creation. They are finding design and order to be more the norm, confusion, and disorder to less likely be the cause behind the created world around us. Again, do not expect to see this in the evening news or front-page headlines. Again, while widely known in scientific circles but deliberately kept from the public, evidence in the secular world supporting, "Intelligent Design" is growing and continuing to come in, while evidence continues to mount against the "so called" theory of evolution. While its credibility continues to evaporate, men of truth are uncovering more evidence the theory was a fraud, nothing more than a series of speculations and elaborate hoaxes perpetrated on the gullible and unsuspecting. Its theories and guesses are proving to be nothing more than junk science at best, and a great conspiracy designed to deceive the masses at worst. Its whole basis rest on the writings of a man who lived over a hundred years ago, surely man has learned more since Darwin authored his book.

> *Having no basis in reality or fact, Evolution is a major arm and core staple of the seed of darkness. The idea that man is a product of evolution, and is on his way to godhood, is the foundation stone of the "Big Lie."*

Many men have made claims to having found "the missing link," but all of them have turned out to be either false links or hoaxes. The missing link is still missing, for one reason, it never existed there never has been a missing link." At their core, those who promote this lie cannot tolerate the thought of a personal loving Creator as the One behind Creation. These are people under the sway and power of Satan. They do not know it; many of them do not believe he exists, so the last place they would ever look for him is in themselves. Remember, "We don't fight against flesh and blood."

Thus, they are hell-bent on a mission to debunk any notion of the Scriptures being the truth, as shown in their doctrine of moral relativism, and "no moral absolutes." To show you just how confused their thinking is, even the statement *"No Moral Absolutes"* is a contradiction in and of itself and cannot be true. To them everything is gray, and it depends; in their worldview there is no black and white, everything is relative.

But let us briefly list some of their other tools: diversity, affirmative action, sensitivity training, tolerance, conflict resolution, gaslighting, censorship, multiculturalism, wokeism, and the daddy of them all Political Correctness. As so many things twisted, these doctrines of demons use a form of manipulation (witchcraft), designed to pressure people into conformity or face ridicule, intimidation, or mockery by example. The goal is to replace the Word of God with the traditions of men. The unspoken implication is, "act like this." Have you ever seen or had exposure to any of these? We used to call it brainwashing.

Just think, if they could just get rid of the God of the Bible, the God of the Christians, think of the freedom, think of the things they could do, without stigma and guilt. They could marry a member of the same sex; they could even marry 3, 4, even 5 other people, or even an animal (a favorite pet). Free from convicting guilt, where does it end pedophilia, euthanasia, abortion on demand, wait a minute, some of this is already legal. The people behind these doctrines have fellowship with demons, they see themselves as having superior intellect, believing they are the anointed, and the wise ones who alone should decide what men should know and believe. They have come a long way to set themselves as the arbiters of truth. Having believed the lie, "You will be like God knowing good and evil," they have a god complex, and want to control and dictate the thoughts and opinions of the masses.

> *"Surely you have things turned around! Shall the Potter be esteemed as the clay; for shall the thing made say of Him Who made it," "He did not make me?" Or shall the thing formed say of Him Who formed it, "He has no understanding"?[9]*

Junk science has proven to be a useful tool in promoting the deceptions of this group of Liberal, Atheist, Communist, Socialist, Relativist, Evolutionist, Secularist, Internationalist, and all other forms of God haters. They seek power for themselves by promoting a godless view of the world.

The PR campaign of this group is without equal. For years, they have used professionally sounding, authoritative spokespeople who say in fact what they know or should have known to be untrue. They have positioned themselves as men of knowledge, wisdom, and understanding. Besides the "doctrines of demons" cited above, we note some of the attention-grabbing props they have used: Charts showing the stages of evolution; bones of dead men and animals; radiometric dating and Carbon–14 testing, and now computer animations.

> *These are the people, "always learning and never able to come to the knowledge of the truth."[10] Their willful presumptions have gone unchallenged, until recently. Many social media platforms, podcasts, talk radio, as public outlets are exposing the charade. Through them, many people are hearing truth or having confirmed things that they for a longtime have either thought or suspected, and those of a temporal secular mind-set hate it.*

CHAPTER 16

Genome Coding: By Design

Then God said, "Let the earth bring forth the living creature according to its kind: cattle and creeping thing and beast of the earth, each according to its kind;" and it was so. And God made the beast of the earth according to its kind, cattle according to its kind, and everything that creeps on the earth according to its kind. And God saw that it was good.[1]

The National Aeronautical and Space Administration (NASA) use to receive (spend) billions of dollars in money out of the public treasury (taxes) to develop spacecraft and various payloads, sent into outer space. The smartest minds of men were behind these projects. Stated in their vision and mission statements were the goals of discovering the origins and existence of life in places outside the earth. For example, their Vision statement said, "To improve life here, to extend life to there, to find life beyond." While the Mission statement said, "To understand and protect our home planet, to explore the universe and search for life, to inspire the next generation of explorers… as only NASA can."

This is a revealing and shameful exposure showing just how far man has come in denying truth's that anyone of us can wake-up here on earth and see every day. For God is not far away, the truth is not out there, it is right here on earth, and all around us for those who want to know Him. As strange as it may sound, the real goal is not to find proof that He exists, for we find that right here on earth, the real goal is to prove that He does not.

We saw the excitement as scientists raced to be the first in mapping the Human Genome, *deciphering the DNA Code*, to discover the genetic makeup of the human body. But is it not a wonder that few of these researchers has ever stopped to ask, "How did the programming (the code) get there?"

Let us look at an analogy; "If Astronauts had landed on the surface of Mars, in hopes of finding signs of life at some point, stumbled across a notebook-sized case partially buried in the Martian soil, we would all hear the news of this incredible discovery. While digging it up, to their surprise, they discovered that it bore a strong likeness to a laptop computer, and it still worked, yet it had unique keys and foreign symbols different from anything men had ever seen. Would they assume that it was just another feature of the Martian landscape, or would they hail this as a sign of intelligent life?

First, they would know that someone made it and would naturally begin a search of discovery; they would naturally ask, "Who made it?" How did it get there, what do the keys, and foreign symbols mean? If ever we had a compelling case for the existence of a Creator, if believers ever had an opportunity to show proof of His existence, the discovery of the "Genome code" and the miracles performed by DNA would be it. If the skeptic ever needed proof of the existence of God, DNA is that proof. Yet consider the implications of this discovery, how the media released this information to the public.

The silence of those who perform research into the mysteries of God's Creation is "deafening," "O the hypocrisy of it all!"

"They continue to repress and hinder the knowledge of the Truth." Is it not their goal, to keep men in darkness?

Truth is, DNA coding consists of a digital coding system and DNA sequencing is an error correcting, self-replicating process. This could never have happened by accident, or by itself, any more than the computer program that I am using, all by itself, author this book. Birds do not know how to build nests by accident, any more than a colony of ants working together build an elaborate mound by accident. Honeybees go through an untaught ritual to tell other bees where to gather honey as they search for fresh flowers, exchanging pollination for nectar. The Hive works as one to produce the honeycomb. This is to say nothing of the organized methodical order in which any one of these magnificent creations day after day carry on and achieve such great feats, not by accident but by design. Can you guess which of the two seed does not want the truth known, because it does not fit into their plan of a world excluding the God Who Created all things?

"Alas, although the evidence is all around us, these atheist and agnostics are the metaphoric lumbermen, who refuse to see the forest for the trees."

DNA programming, just like computer programming, is not an accident or a fluke of nature, it HAPPENS BY DESIGN, INTELLIGENT DESIGN. Any written work on DNA will involve words like sequence, copy, information, instructions, formation, synthesis, orchestrate, make, direct, task, steps, coding, encoding and noncoding and a host of other innovative words all of which point to intelligence. Anyone working for that company, the name of which starts with an "M," will tell you, without a program and programmer, "It's not going to work." Here what is true of the computer is true of DNA, whether plant or animal, this includes man. All life forms in this present phase of the Plan began by design, with the bodies of all plants, or animal life forms brought into existence by parents with the ability to reproduce after their kind.

In the Creation account of Genesis, in verses 1:11, 12, 21, 24, 25, we read the words *"according to its kind."* God said this of every animated life form created whether plant, bird, sea life, insect, or animal. In addition, when God commanded Noah to bring animals into the Ark, we read the words, *"After their kind, and after its kind."*² DNA researchers recognize (the miracle) the power in seeds, yet none of them dare come forth and admit God's power of bringing forth the various creations after their kind as seen in the book of Genesis.

"Repro-duction," to reproduce. Each creation began with a single cell, "a seed cell," the egg (seed) of the mother, fertilized by the sperm (seed) of the father. DNA is the Master Plan for all earthly life forms; the design of every living creation on earth contained within its intricate and graceful structures.

At conception, egg and sperm combine to form a new "Living Master Seed" (egg cell). This cell now has the life-germ of the parents, plant, or animal (of its kind) and everything needed to reproduce a copy of the original life-form, after its kind, thus the person you see in the mirror. Yet this Master

> DNA IS THE MASTER PLAN FOR ALL EARTHLY LIFE FORMS. AT CONCEPTION, EGG AND SPERM COMBINE TO FORM A NEW LIVING, "MASTER SEED" (EGG CELL).

Seed (egg cell) is so small you can barely see it with the naked eye. If you asked a Botanist the difference between an oak, a palm tree, and lichen, he or she would declare the broadest line of classification separates them from one another. However, if you placed the germs of these plants before them, to choose one from the other, they could not do it. Even under the most powerful microscope, they would yield no clue, and if analyzed by a chemist they would keep their secret. The same is true of the Master Seed, the life-germ of the various animals and man.

No one can tell which is which, or what makes these tiny little specks no larger than a pinhead grow into the millions of distinct species of creatures? What is there that the eye cannot see that decides which of the many creatures it will be? Only a Being of infinite intelligence, a Designer Creator, could have made such unfailing laws of reproduction, each after its kind. Just think, from that single cell came every new cell that went into making your body. Estimates are the average adult human body has from 10 to 100 Trillion (100,000,000,000,000) cells.

The cells multiply by dividing, each holding the first DNA program, however, with slight changes making each cell unique. The whole procedure and design are genius, requiring intelligence far beyond the abilities of the smartest of men, let alone brute nature. Initially in the womb, and afterward outside the womb, this procedure went on and on until you, your whole body became complete. Each created life form with its many cell types and instructions came from one Master Seed. The size of a pinhead, yet it's estimated the information if written could easily fill over 20 full encyclopedia sets; the drawback, the text would be so small, you would need a microscope to read it.

All of this has parallels and reminds us of how the Body of Christ develops. Each believer is like a cell of His body, a body which itself multiplies through spreading the Gospel, the Good News. This is the work that Christ began in forming the Church, which is His body. The Apostle Paul used a similar analogy in describing how members of the body strengthened the Church and promoted her growth. He said, "For as we have many members in one body, but all the members do not have the same function, so we, being many, are one body in Christ, and individually members of one another.

Having then gifts differing according to the grace that is given to us, let us use them; if *prophecy*, let us prophesy in proportion to our faith; or *ministry*, let us use it in our ministering; he who *teaches*, in teaching; he who *exhorts*, in exhortation; he who *gives*, with liberality; he who *leads*, with diligence; he who shows *mercy*, with cheerfulness." [3] Given the parallels, a study of the seven gifts identified above and how they compare to the workings of the various systems of the human body might yield some interesting results and insights. In his first letter to the Church at Corinth he wrote, "For as the body is one and has many members, but all the members of that one body, being many, are one body, so also is Christ. For by one Spirit we were all baptized into one body—whether Jews or Greeks, whether slaves or free—and have all been made to drink into one Spirit. For in fact the body is not one member but many. [4] He follows up in 1Corinthians 12:15-31, where he addresses purposes and roles in the body of Christ. The cells in the body know their purpose; they know how to produce new cells. They know what position and roles to take on within the various body systems as they replace those that have become old, damaged, or have died; this is all done "by design," without our conscious awareness. As the body produces new cells, each new cell knows its purpose and role in the body of each life form. Each cell works to form various body parts, internal organs, and systems, which serve distinct roles in support of the whole body, the final product.

As Believers, we have a place in His Body.

Now, of the trillions of cells that make you, you, your body works to keep you looking like you by replacing damaged or dead cells with new ones, which we call healing. Just as captivating, scientists have known for some time now the body molders, and that cells constantly reproduce new ones replacing old, dying, and damaged ones, thus we get a new body every seven years. For example, take a damaged fingernail, by DNA programming cells know how to configure themselves. The cells that grow to heal the fingernail will not become a skin or muscle cell, but a new fingernail cell. The cells communicate; they have internal programming, they know what to be in composition; whether skin, bone,

> IT'S AS IF THE WHOLE BODY IS LIKE A MAP, WITH EACH SPECIFIC CELL POSITION HAVING AN ADDRESS, POSITION, OR NUMBER.

cartilage, muscle, or one of the major organs. It is as if the whole body is like a map, with each specific cell position having an address, position, or number. Not only do they know this, but they also know how and where to position themselves when replacing old, damaged, or dead cells, so in purpose, appearance, bodily role, with all the changes and inner workings, you still look like you. The DNA of every living cell, whether plant or animal, needs hardware and software.

Even in the natural realm there must be an intelligent ordering and organizing of the material (dirt) to build the life form, plant, or animal. Stated another way, to run properly there must be a program, and thus a Programmer, we can now see this in computers; however, in created life forms the software not only supports the life form—it builds it.

Jesus said, "It is written, 'Man shall not live by bread alone, but by every word that proceeds from the mouth of God.'"5

Where is the support for evolution?

Those who subscribe to the theory of Evolution want you to believe that "Life began with simple living forms on their own becoming more complex, through a series of natural selection and mutations." This idea of natural selection is a red herring, for any practice of choice assumes life and intelligence. All life forms on the earth emanate from the earth, made of earthly stuff. The theory of evolution assumes life, an inherent intelligence exists within a handful of dirt (Intelligent living Dirt), and new life forms somehow *miraculously* sprang from it, how ridiculous this is. On the other hand, the problem with mutations is that they have never produced anything of lasting benefit in Creation. A mutation reveals the cell lacks proper coding, or some of the coding information (the program) is missing. In the Bible, defects, sickness, disease, and death are attributable to sin.

Because cells are whole organisms, with the potential of passing on abnormalities to the next generation; in childbirth whenever something goes wrong in the baby's growth and development, it is a genetic or birth defect. Extreme abnormalities classified as syndromes, disorders, or mutations. In the past, men futilely tried to crossbreed species, the tries failed because of defective or incompatible DNA, which often produced sterile offspring, incapable of reproducing a healthy new life.

Take the mutation known as "Cancer," even cancer cells have all the information needed to grow and destroy healthy cells. When it comes to the body, the medical community has found what they consider "the norm." These consist of bodily signs and chemical balances based on what they call baselines, any deviations from these they consider abnormal. This is what medical science tries to treat. Therefore, medical science does not support evolution. Again, if it evolved at what point does it complete the end state, when does it become fixed and stable?

If evolution is still going on, when will we see the next step? Of the many conditions needed to carry on life on earth as we now see and know it, the evolutionist argument is that time, and this impersonal force called "Nature," created and produced all life, by accident, this is offensive. On another point, the fossil record does not support evolution, nor can it, meantime, they keep looking. It is not for the lack of money, billions of dollars and untold thousands of hours of research have gone into trying to prove this false theory.

There must be many conditions conducive to life, and for life to continue. In the world, we see many natural, physical laws and rules governing the various features of life, making the earth life centric; the basic building blocks in matter and chemistry, the exact and self-sustaining balances needed for a life-supporting atmosphere. This does not include a multitude of checks and balances, cycles and seasons, the exact distance of the earth in its orbit around the sun, or the orbit of the moon. All kept animated with such precision that man can know the actual length of a year, down to a nano-second. The number of things needed obviously goes beyond the scope of this work. Yet like a fine jeweler's watch, take anyone of them away and you no longer have life, again is it life by chance, or by design?

Mysteries of the Creation

Man through observation has learned much about the works of the Creator. He has learned to harness and use many things in Creation for his own benefit. However, there are many things that man has little or no idea, either where they originate, or exactly what makes them work. For example, "Gravity," how does it work? "Electricity," where does it originate? These are still mysteries. Another example is how does "Water" manage to keep its properties, this is another mystery, and we have new mysteries revealing themselves all the time.

However, the main mystery is "life itself," without this one we have nothing. All the necessary parts can be in place, but without the principle of life at work, all you have is a corpse, or an outer shell. In the Creation account, Adam did not become Adam until after God breathed into his lifeless casing the "Breath of lives."

You might ask, what does a search for secrets in the depths of outer space, or a search into the innermost secrets of men's hearts, or even a search into the micro miniature world of nature has to do with the Master's Plan? The point is this; while we see evidence proving the existence of the Creator, all around us, men will not find him by searching, no matter how hard they try. This is a spiritual thing, and the spiritually dead and blind cannot find Him because they do not look for Him, in the place that He told us we could find Him, in His Word.

Without God man would not exist, without God, man is without a clue.

CHAPTER 17

Two Seed

For whoever wants to save his higher, spiritual, eternal life, will lose it the lower, natural, temporal life which is lived only on earth; and whoever gives up his life which is lived only on earth for My sake and the Gospel's will save it his higher, spiritual life in the eternal kingdom of God. For what does it profit a man to gain the whole world, and forfeit his life in the eternal kingdom of God? For what can a man give as an exchange, compensation, a ransom, in return for his blessed life in the eternal kingdom of God? [1]

CAIN AND ABEL

By various accounts and illustrations, God's Word has given many examples and warnings about the two natures living within men; we see it from the beginning in the lives of Cain and Abel. By natural birth, men are in sin and the subjects of Satan, that old serpent called the Devil. By new birth, men become the sons of God. We see these two natures at war with one another on the earth.

"In Him" we have peace, because of the Truth that He has given us, in the world we will have tribulation; but be of good cheer, for He has overcome the world. [2]

"The Prince of Peace," Jesus said, "I did not come to bring peace but a sword." The Message of "the Cross" is divisive, it cuts clean between those who accept and those who reject God's Master Plan. It separates the two seed, dividing humanity into two classes, the seed of the woman, and the seed of the serpent, the saved, and the lost, "the Wheat and the Tares." As already mentioned, in this present world God tests and Satan tempts. God tests a man to help him come to faith so he might take and eat of the tree of life. Satan tempts the same man to reject Christ as the source of life and content himself with the knowledge of good and evil, and his life in this present age, without Christ. These are the representative types, the good and bad seed, "the good and bad trees, the good and bad fruit, and the sheep and the goats."

Critical key to understanding the Plan

A critical key to understanding the Plan is to recognize there are two plans, the Master Plan and the enemy's plan.

The will and plan of the enemy of life is that humanity seek all our pleasure in, and fix our heartfelt hopes on, this present Age over which he presides, as the god of this Age. That men use their best endeavors, by various sensuous and intellectual occupations and delights, and countless ways of killing time, which he has provided, to keep our thoughts from ever wandering over into that, "Age to come." That Age will find him a fettered captive, instead of a prince, and a god.

SOWING AND REAPING

Sowing and Reaping is one of the most powerful principles found in the Word of God. As men begin to understand the nature of what God did in Creation, they are seeing more of the inherent power contained within seeds. As we said, DNA is the "Master Plan" of physical life. Within each primary seed is the germ of life having all the instructions; the program and miniature cellular factories, all designed to gather and produce a final product. We see this in plants, in animals, in sea life, in birds and in man, all producing life after its kind.

From a single cell, "a miniature factory," the whole plant or animal creation grows and unfolds, forming the whole creation with all its various parts. Try this; imagine a seed, which could grow into a house, a car, or a small airplane. Imagine taking this seed, planting it in your backyard, each day going out and watering it; in time you watch it unfold and grow into the complete house, car, or small airplane, with all the optional features. Just think, when you look at either plant or animal creations, this in effect, is what God has done.

In the plant kingdom, seeds take root and grow out of the fertile ground. In the animal kingdom, the seed attaches itself to the fertile womb forming an umbilical cord through which the new life form receives the blood of life support, nourishment. Thus, everything needed to develop into an infant, or smaller, still maturing copy of the parents. We also see this same characteristic in creatures hatched from eggs; these parallels are not accidental.

*N*ow, let us look at a spiritual example, found in the fifteenth Chapter of John, "Christ teaching on the true Vine." The Husbandman is the Father; Christ is the Vine, and individual Believers the branches. The illustration shows the umbilical (spiritual), connection between Christ and His Church, thus revealing how Believers grow, and bear fruit. Take and break a branch off a growing vine, cast it aside, and come back a day later, you will find a withered, dead branch. As it is in the physical, so it is in the spiritual with our life in Christ. It is the life of Christ working through the Holy Spirit in the believer, which produces the fruit, for Jesus, taught this saying, "Without Me you can do nothing." [3]

Life is in the blood, the Spirit is life, It is the lifeblood in the Believer, "It is the Spirit Who gives life; the flesh *profits nothing*. The words that I speak to you are spirit, and they are life." [4]

> *"Life is in the blood!"* [5] *God revealed this to Noah, over 4,000 years ago. Blood provides the oxygen and nutrients needed to support the cells of the body.*

In Chapter 13, we looked at our life here being the second stage of the journey. In this life, we sow, and we reap. It is here, through sowing, that we decide where we end in the final stage of the journey.

> *The Account of the Vine (John 15:1-17); The Parable of the Sower; (Matthew 13:1-9); and the Unjust Steward (Luke 16:1-13), all point to this.*

This is where we see the mystery of the seed, the next stage in our real evolution. If we die to self, putting off the old physical nature, and the things of this world, figuratively buried with Him in His death; we will be born again, and in fact born in His likeness, in the resurrection. This is sowing and reaping.

Through the Seed of His Word, we achieve the final makeover, taking on the new (spiritual) nature. Thus, we see the contrast and reason for the conflict between the two natures. For, "the one who SOWS to please his sinful NATURE, from that NATURE will REAP destruction; the one who sows to please the Spirit, from the Spirit will REAP ETERNAL LIFE." [5]

Here our lives are like seeds. The fruit of seeds sown in this life will display themselves in the harvest, the life to come. My hope and prayer are that you get this and know that God gave you the promise of life, "And although one day, they place your lifeless body in the ground, you're not dead, you will rise again." So, when it comes to Sowing and Reaping you might say:

"Sown in the Heart, Reaped in Life. Sown in Life, Reaped in the Harvest."

Again, about the Truth of our resurrection, the Holy Spirit expecting questions wrote through the Apostle Paul saying, "But someone may ask, "How will the dead be raised? What kind of bodies will they have?" What a foolish question! When you put a seed into the ground, it does not grow into a plant unless it dies first. And what you put in the ground is not the plant that will grow, but only a dry little seed of wheat or whatever it is you are planting. Then God gives it a new body—just the kind He wants it to have. A different kind of plant grows from each kind of seed.[6]

The Lord revealed the mystery of this principle, of His death producing life being comparable to seed. Thus, we see the principle is true in not only the natural world but the spiritual as well. For Jesus replied, "The time has come for the Son of Man to enter into His glory."

The truth is, "a kernel of wheat must be planted in the soil. Unless it dies it will be alone—a single seed. But its death will produce many new kernels—a plentiful harvest of new lives. Those who love their life in this world will lose it. Those who despise their life in this world will keep it for eternal life."[7] It was His death and resurrection, which caused many to look to Him for eternal life. When we die to self and live for Him, we have His desire to tell others about the Good News.

By looking at the lifestyle choices around us, we see those who have placed all their hopes and dreams in this the temporal world, and those who have placed their hopes and dreams in Christ and the world to come. Together they make clear the two perspectives and worldviews held by humanity.

While some things are temporary, others are eternal. God has given His Word to help us choose and then tell others the difference between this temporal and the eternal. His Word shows many examples of those sowing to the flesh, reaping corruption, and those sowing to the Spirit, and reaping Eternal Life. This is going on right now for, "Even now the reaper draws his wages, even now he harvests the crop for eternal Life, so that the sower and the reaper may be glad together."[8]

Two Seed–Confirmation

Understanding there are two seed which make up humanity is essential to understanding the Plan. Those who lean toward the fleshly, the temporal nature, and those who lean toward the spiritual, the eternal. One worldview embraces death, the other life. One group cannot see there is an ordered and organized Plan to test man here on earth, during this time on probation and the other group can.

This is the reason that Believers need to know the truth, for in this present generation the Children of darkness are more shrewd in their dealings than the Children of light.[9] An example of this is the secular domination and stronghold over public education. While education should be *open* to discovery, Secularism has forcefully mandated the use of public funds to indoctrinate all children into the temporal minded religion of evolution, with its entire host of damning doctrines.

To support their twisted doctrines and stand against Christianity, some say since science has not accepted, the Christian belief of "Creation and Intelligent Design," it cannot be true. They would have us forget that these spokespersons for science are but men.

Truth is, outside the revelations given in the Bible, they have no way of answering questions such as, "How did life begin? Did God create man? Did He create man for a purpose? Did God visit man in the form of His Son Jesus Christ?" Nevertheless, it reveals where men have placed their faith. Not only do they reject the alternate views of Creation and Intelligent Design despite all the proof, but they also fervently fight against them, because they do not conform to the secularist mind-set and worldview. The only alternatives allowed are ones that support their temporal agenda. If only Believers were more forceful and shrewd in presenting the truth.

Going from Temporal to Eternal:

The human body (the flesh) is a temporal housing for the soul and spirit of man. Man's physical body consist of dust animated by God's Spirit, dust taken from and supported by the earth and water.

God gave the choice of life or death to the first man Adam. It was the "Fall," which delivered all flesh over to disease, decay, death, and corruption. After the Fall, God said to man, "In the sweat of your face shall you eat bread until you return to the ground, for out of it you were taken; for dust you are and to dust you shall return." [10]

Since the beginning, with Adam and Eve, male or female, each of our lives bear record to the temporal nature of the flesh, and the likelihood of anyone of us dying is still 100 percent. All life on earth in this present Creation consist of transformed, animated water and dust, therefore from dust we come to dust we return. Job said, "All flesh would perish together, and man would turn again to dust."[11] While the Preacher, Solomon said, "All go to one place: all are from the dust, and all return to dust."[12] And, "Then shall the dust out of which God made man's body return to the earth as it was, and the spirit shall return to God Who gave it."[13]

Row after row, marker after marker, the Earth laden with countless tombs, is ever sighing for credulity. Ocean, as his chasing waves roll over the bones of multitudes lying amid their unheeded treasures, moans in response. And Hades, his vast realms peopled daily by fresh colonies of unclothed spirits, solemnly proclaim that God is true.

Adam and Christ Contrasted

When Adam sinned, sin entered the entire human race and "look at the results." Adam's sin brought death, so death spread to everyone, for everyone sinned. Yes, people sinned even before God gave the law. And though there was no law to break, since it had not yet been given, they all died anyway—even though they did not disobey an explicit commandment of God, as Adam did. What a contrast between Adam and Christ, who was yet to come! And what a difference between our sin and God's generous gift of forgiveness. For this one man, Adam, brought death to many through his sin. But this other man, Jesus Christ, brought forgiveness to many through God's bountiful gift. And the result of God's gracious gift is vastly different from the result of that one man's sin.

For Adam's sin led to condemnation, but we have the gift of being accepted by God, even though we are guilty of many sins. The sin of this one man, Adam, caused death to rule over us, but all who receive God's wonderful, gracious gift of righteousness will live in triumph over sin and death through this one man, Jesus Christ. Yes, Adam's one sin brought condemnation upon everyone, but Christ's one act of righteousness makes all people right in God's sight and gives them life. Because one-person disobeyed God, many people became sinners. But because one other person obeyed God, many people will be made right in God's sight. God's law was given so that all people could see how sinful they were. But as people sinned increasingly, God's wonderful kindness became more abundant.

So just as sin ruled over all people and brought them to death, now God's wonderful kindness rules instead, giving us right standing with God and resulting in eternal life through Jesus Christ our Lord.[14]

There is a clear contrast between the temporal (flesh) and the eternal (spirit) natures. The Apostle Paul wrote further, "But *if Christ lives in you, then although* your *natural* body is dead by reason of sin and guilt, the spirit is alive because of *the* righteousness *that He imputes to you.* And if the Spirit of Him Who raised up Jesus from the dead dwells in you, *then* He Who raised up Christ Jesus from the dead will also restore to life your mortal (short-lived, perishable) bodies through His Spirit Who dwells in you. So then, brethren, we are debtors, but not to the flesh, we are not bound to our carnal nature, to live a life ruled by the standards set up by the flesh. For if you live according to *the dictates of* the flesh, you will surely die. But if through the power of the *Holy* Spirit you are *habitually* putting to death (making extinct, deadening) the *evil* deeds prompted by the body, you shall *really and genuinely* live forever."[15]

Therefore, there are the two kinds of people in the world today, those who enter through the narrow gate, and those on the broad way. Those who enter the broad gate, the broad road, live life in a temporary context, living only for the pleasures and joys of the moment, they treasure and adorn the outer man of the flesh. While Believers having knowledge of the temporal and the eternal, *the old and new,* they have chosen the "one way," the narrow gate of life; the narrow-minded have taken the eternal perspective. They have renounced the joys and pleasures of "sin for a season," for a reason. They live to adorn to mature and beautify the inner man of the spirit, through fellowship with God's Spirit. They recognize that this is not our home, this is not our world, and "we're only pilgrims and strangers, passing through." They realize that God knows everything about our journey here on earth, and the book written about our life now stands unveiled in Heaven. They are the born again, their names written in the Lamb's Book of Life. They believe that Jesus Christ is alive in Heaven right now, and He will come again to receive His own from the earth. While He is away, He has called us to continue in His service. The goal of this work is to encourage believers to continue that work.

> "If any man serve Me, let him follow Me; and where I am, there shall also My servant be:
>
> if any man serve Me, him will My Father honor." [16]

CHAPTER 18

Two Views

Do not be fooled by those who say such things, for "bad company corrupts good character."[1]

Woe to those who call evil good, and good evil; Who put darkness for light, and light for darkness; Who put bitter for sweet, and sweet for bitter?[2]

THE TWO VIEWS, TEMPORAL AND ETERNAL LIFE

We see the brevity of this life when we consider just how short our life here is. One reason for our being here is to reproduce the race. Now, according to the temporal minded view, we live life in three boxes: "Learn, Earn, and Retire." As children, *we learned*. As young and middle-aged adults, we work, *earn*, raise families, and spend most of our lifetime, 30 to 40 years, in various careers raising and supporting those families, and then *we retire*. Afterwards we then spend the rest of our days waiting for death. Our role in this life is to reproduce and take care of our young until they can take care of themselves. During this lifetime, the focus of many is on temporal things and events, which tie us to this temporal experience.

We learn, develop, and conform our understanding of life only as good as those who have influenced our education and learning. However, if all we have ever learned is what the temporal minded have taught us, is it any wonder that so many cling so tightly to a temporal worldview; it is only natural, right? We have all had common experiences, which influence, affect, and condition the way that we see the world, those influences come through family, friends, relatives, community, media, the academic world, government, and some form of religion. We have all experienced some form of conditioning, conditioning that makes it unthinkable for many to ask, *is there more.* You ask why this is a problem. The problem is this, while people can describe and respond to the things of this world; when it comes to anything beyond this, somehow the answers fall short. It is because of a restricted mind-set, a temporal over eternal, that people bound in the world and this present age cannot see anything beyond.

It is clear there are two worldviews and two voices out there, two visions of the future; one contained in God's Word, and one held by the secular mind-set. For secularists deny any truth, which does not fit neatly into their ordered "little box of reality," of what the world should be. Those who believe in this way are neither intelligent nor wise. Like those who live out their lives in the Matrix (the movie) a veil blocks their understanding, and they are unable to see the Plan and Work of God, or the work of the enemies of their soul. As the Scriptures says, *while declaring to be wise they became fools,* FOR IT IS WRITTEN: "I will destroy the wisdom of the wise; the intelligence of the intelligent I will frustrate."[3]

The Eternal View

For those of us whose eyes are open, everything in Creation shows Intelligent Design, and the interconnectedness of life, with all the parts working to support life. The earth is the only planet in this solar system that has this leaning toward life; earth is *life centric,* by design, having a substantial number of integrated systems, which all work to support life. This is a given, proved by the fact the earth has such an abundance of life. We find life in various sceneries and settings. Life all around us did not come into existence by accident.

What the Temporal can't See

Nevertheless, because of the abundance alone, life in the eyes of some is cheap and of little value. How did it get here? As a rule, and contrary to what the atheist and God haters would have us believe, *"life has to beget life."* Again, this might come as a shock to them, but dead things have never produced life; they never will, and there is no such thing as *intelligent dirt.* This is all common sense; yet Believers find themselves in opposition against those whose words and actions point to the depth of conditioning, which they want these lies assimilated into the social well of public thinking. When they argue against obvious truth, they reveal that they are living in a dream world, "a Matrix," a warped reality where everything is fictional.

Each of us carries a perspective whether temporal or eternal, which will affect our outlook, our disposition, our attitude, and our belief. From the secularist worldview, science cannot be wrong. In their eyes, man and not God is the center of it all. They are quick to dismiss any truth, which shakes or challenges their worldview. They would rather we live in their world of dreams, as opposed to having someone step forward and admit the truth. Frankly, it has gotten that bad, but again, this only serves to confirm the Word of Truth. Caught in a delusion they would have us all share their worldview, rather than see the obvious, which for the seeing is as plain as the nose on your face. Some ask, "Would they deliberately keep the truth from us." Truth is many scientists, politicians, and educators are just like any other man, they are men of sight, and not men of faith, excluding a few, many are secular, holding a temporal worldview. It is impossible for those holding a temporal worldview to have an eternal mind-set; they cannot see it. It is impossible for faith to live within the minds of those who live in and only for this present age. The temporal minded focus on the material, the eternal minded the spiritual. All they have is what they imagine beyond this life. Now if the earth is life centric having a tendency toward life, then why are so many secularists hell-bent on promoting a culture of death, a view of the world that just does not make sense.

> CAUGHT IN A DELUSION THEY WOULD HAVE US ALL SHARE THEIR WORLDVIEW, RATHER THAN SEE THE OBVIOUS, WHICH FOR THE SEEING IS AS PLAIN AS THE NOSE ON YOUR FACE.

Does this not confirm the fact there are two seeds? The temporal minded, on the broad road, see this life as a dead end. While the eternal minds see this life as a stage in the journey, a narrow road leading to a real, never-ending, eternal life. The differences in these two worldviews are as different as day and night. "Temporal mindedness destroys eternal potential." Throughout human history, the enemy has seduced the temporal minded by the lust of pleasure, sex, and power. Eternal minded value relationships, which help us love people over our stuff. People with a temporal mind-set have nothing, their motivation revealed by the need to have power and control things. People with an eternal mind-set realize that "in Christ" they own all things; their motivation revealed by the need to love, "God is Love," and He owns all things.

THE PARABLE OF THE WHEAT AND THE TARES

In the Parable of "the Wheat and the Tares," who do you think Jesus was talking about, and how did He show them?

Another parable He put forth to them, saying: *"The kingdom of heaven is like* a man who sowed good seed in his field; but while men slept, his enemy came and sowed tares among the wheat and went his way. But when the grain had sprouted and produced a crop, *then the tares also appeared.* So, the servants of the owner came and said to him, 'Sir, did you not sow good seed in your field?' How then does it have tares?' He said to them, *'An enemy has done this.'* The servants said to him, 'Do you want us then to go and gather them up?' But he said, 'No, lest while you gather up the tares you also uproot the wheat with them." *Let both grow together until the harvest,* and at the time of harvest I will say to the reapers, "First gather together the tares and bind them in bundles to burn them but gather the wheat into my barn.""⁴

The Parable of the Tares Explained

"Then Jesus sent the multitude away and went into the house. And His disciples came to Him, saying, Explain to us the Parable of the tares of the field.' He answered and said to them: 'He who sows the good seed is the Son of Man. The field is the world, the good seeds are the sons of the kingdom, but the tares are the sons of the wicked one. The enemy who sowed them is the Devil, the harvest is the end of the Age, and the reapers are the angels. Therefore, as the tares are gathered and burned in the fire, it will be at *the end of this Age.* The Son of Man will send out His angels, and they will gather out of His kingdom all things that offend, and those who practice lawlessness, and will cast them into the furnace of fire. There will be wailing and gnashing of teeth. Then the righteous will shine forth as the sun in the kingdom of their Father. He who has ears to hear, let him hear!'"⁵

The parable of "the Wheat and the Tares" teaches that as the time for the harvest approaches the differences between the wheat and the tares will become more strikingly and clearly shown and obvious. This conflict between good and evil will last "until the Harvest, which is the end of this Age." And as soon as the wheat, "the Church," is ripe, the last member coming into the body, Jesus will come back to gather His wheat at "the Rapture."

Yet the words, "gather the tares, and bind them in bundles, to burn them, but gather the wheat into my barn." Confused, some claim the

Church is to remain on earth until the "Tares" are burned, calling for the Church to go through, "the Tribulation." However, *"before,"* the harvest of the wheat, they gathered the "Tares" in "bundles," not to burn them but to have them, *"separated"* and ready to burn *"after"* they garner the wheat into the "Heavenly barn." This gathering of the "tares" into bundles is now going on in the false religions of Marxism, Socialism, Liberalism and Secular Humanism, Islam, New Age, and any other organized belief's, which deny that Jesus is the Christ. This Parable teaches the "Wheat," and the "Tares" will be inseparable, until the end of this present Dispensation.

LIBERALS DECLARE WAR ON THE UNITED STATES

Who are the "Tares?" We know who planted them.

After years of suffering persecution under the Church of England, Believers, by the hand of God's providence, came to this continent to found a new nation called America. It seems that what God had in mind was a nation that would be a light to the world, and an example of His blessings on those whose God is the Lord. America prospered and grew; God gave many blessings on her and made her a blessing to all nations on the earth. However, as she began to turn her back and forgot the God Who poured out blessings and grace on her, the nation began to experience problems. An enemy born and bred from within infiltrated her. From "before" the 1960's, which saw the decadence of the peace movement with its rallies, demonstrations, drugs, and free love orgies, organizers were secretly meeting and strategizing ways to destroy the nation from within.

Of God, Job said, "He raises up nations, and He destroys them. He makes nations expand, and He abandons them."[6]

Here we see how the enemy planted the Tares. Marxist, Socialist, and Communist sympathizers with their atheistic beliefs invaded college campuses across the nation with a mission to indoctrinate and inculcate a whole generation, which at a critical time in history had begun to lose its way. Incited by the "Tares" of atheists, they began to ask questions. This generation found rebellion to be an acceptable response against authority and all the rules of society, which they felt had failed to give them real answers to the purpose and meaning of life.

"The Church was fast asleep," while a generation in rebellion expressed themselves through sex, drugs, and rock and roll. The enemy had planted

many seeds of dissension, seeds that began to grow a culture in rebellion on campuses all around the country that would forever change this nation. That generation sought every form of rebellion imaginable, in clothes, in hair, in lifestyle, in demonstrations and rebellion against authority. Now, the students of the sixties are the civil, social, and political leaders of today. Behind the veil, this was a spiritual attack waged by the forces of the enemy to subvert a Christian nation through the doctrines and teachings of demons. When you look at what they attacked and how it brought about the simultaneous subversion of a whole generation, this was not an accident; it was an organized campaign. Can you see how we got here? But what happened? The Church and Nation were being seduced, *"An enemy has done this."*

> THIS GENERATION FOUND REBELLION TO BE AN ACCEPTABLE RESPONSE, AGAINST AUTHORITY AND ALL THE RULES OF A SOCIETY, WHICH THEY FELT, HAD FAILED TO GIVE THEM REAL ANSWERS TO THE PURPOSE AND MEANING OF LIFE.

When the Church in America found the good life, she began, unwittingly, to yield up her weapons, which were the source of her strength and power; she relaxed her weapons of prayer, faith, and the Word of God. Through voluntary disarmament, she forgot her need to be diligent, to watch, and pray. The watchmen left the walls to enjoy the spoils of the good life. Many souls taken captive, a whole generation murdered through abortion, not to mention the other atrocities in decadent living, the fruit of which we are continuing to reap. Spiritually, having sown to the wind, we are now reaping a whirlwind of evil, because we failed to be diligent in guarding our heritage.

Again, during the 1960's, not recognizing the attack of the enemy, the faith of the Church began to wane, and she began to unarm herself; one of the first blows to the Church came against Prayer. Men outlawed God and Prayer, in the public square, arena and in public education, sadder still prayer declined in the Church, at the same time secular media began to ask, *"is God alive," "does He even exist,"* they even spawned, a "God is dead movement?" Intrigued by the world, the Church began to wane. Instead of actively reforming the world with the Gospel, under seduction, she began to copy and subscribe to a philosophy of "go along to get along, and don't rock the boat." Through the progression of subtle seductions, deceptions, and pride, some in the Church began to buy into the LIE. The Church was losing her salt, and just as Jesus had said, "Salt having lost its flavor is good for nothing but to be cast out and trampled under the foot of men."[7]

Having become undiscerning, self-reliant, and self-confident, some began to question their belief in the God of the Bible; others no longer upheld the need to fight. Members of the body began to forget the call to be separated (set apart) from the world. The god of mammon, prosperity, and material gain, slowly at first, replaced the one true God. The Church forgot her call to be salt and light. Like the Nation Israel, She forgot that she served a jealous God who would have no other gods before Him.

Today, we see a divided America, like Moses holding the rod in the battle between Israel and the Amalekites, which we read, "While the people of Israel were still at Rephidim, the warriors of Amalek came to fight against them. Moses commanded Joshua, "Call the Israelites to arms, and fight the army of Amalek. Tomorrow, I will stand at the top of the hill with the staff of God in my hand."

So, Joshua did what Moses had commanded. He led his men out to fight the army of Amalek. Meanwhile Moses, Aaron, and Hur went to the top of a nearby hill. As long as Moses held up the staff with his hands, the Israelites had the advantage. But whenever he lowered his hands, the Amalekites gained the upper hand. Moses' arms finally became too tired to hold up the staff any longer. So, Aaron and Hur found a stone for him to sit on. Then they stood on each side, holding up his hands until sunset. As a result, Joshua and his troops were able to crush the army of Amalek.[8]

The hands that we must hold up now are the hands of prayer.

The Church as salt and light is a preserving influence in the world; after her removal at "the Rapture," there will be nothing to restrain the darkness from overcoming this present evil Age. We know that after the fall of Adam, this world became a Stronghold of Satan, divided into many camps among his principalities and powers. Death and the grave filled, with the souls of many who were the prisoners of this spiritual warfare, captives of the power of Satan. When God pronounced sentence on Creation, He gave the woman the promise of the Redeemer. Jesus has already come to set the

> "THE CHURCH AS SALT AND LIGHT IS A PRESERVING INFLUENCE IN THE WORLD, AFTER HER REMOVAL AT "THE RAPTURE," THERE WILL BE NOTHING TO RESTRAIN THE DARKNESS FROM OVERCOMING THIS PRESENT EVIL AGE."

Captive's free. Today we need a prayer awakening, for a clever enemy is undermining America. When America sent missionaries to foreign countries, there were many reports of signs and wonders; in "His Name" missionaries cast out many demons, but where did they go? Could it be that many of them migrated (if you will) to America. Some believe that these demons, being prisoners on the earth, found a proud and prosperous nation, which had let her guard down and began to seduce her. On arrival, they used the lure of a secular world to captivate and seduce this once God-fearing nation into becoming a place "pox ridden" with many spiritual strongholds. This is causing our nation to become in "type," the Sodom and Gomorrah, which we see today. Some of this is speculation, yet how else can we account for the passive state of the majority. It is as if we were watching a demonic feeding frenzy, a rapid decline in our political, social (moral) values. As the enemy continues to sow seeds of sin and corruption into universal acceptance across the west.

> *If the Church has the potential to affect society for good, then surely the opponents of the Church have the potential to affect it for evil.*

It is becoming clear to many there is a subtle and yet Satanic, pro-evil movement that defies good judgment, and what we use to call common sense, working overtime and overwhelming our nation today. This movement has done its work so subtlety and cunningly that through ignorance and apathy, most in society have not noticed it, or have blown it off as insignificant. Therefore, without much thought, conditioning convinces many to reject its importance or the possibility that it exists.

Nevertheless, we can understand it when we consider the theory of "Gradualism" (the frog in the pot), applied on a supernatural level.

WHAT IS GRADUALISM?

Defined, "Gradualism" is any policy or method used to reach a predetermined end. The enemy does this in stages, by steps or degrees, moving or developing his goals by slight, often-imperceptible change.

The theory of the Frog in the Pot goes like this; take a live frog and place it in a pot of boiling water and at once it jumps out. Now, take the same frog, place it in a cool pot of water, and then slowly turn the temperature up say one degree an hour, before the frog knows it, *"it's too late!"*

America has been on a slow boil as she heads down the road to destruction. Think about it, "Vipers are subtle, but deadly." The reason so many fail to see this as a war is because this conflict is taking place on a spiritual level, beyond the ability of the temporal minded to see and understand. Just as the Word says, "For though we walk in the flesh, we do not war according to the flesh. For the weapons of our warfare *are* not carnal but mighty in God for pulling down strongholds, casting down arguments and every high thing that exalts itself against the knowledge of God, bringing every thought into captivity to the obedience of Christ."[9]

This is a spiritual conflict and therefore we need a Spiritual Awakening. Slowly and gently rocked into a stupor of ignorance and apathy, far too many do not know and do not care.

We need a return to our, "First Love," The Love of seeing His Plan and doing His Will.

Our Prayers are the spiritual weapons in warfare. Like bullets and missiles or the burst of a laser beam, effective prayer having a specific target, always hits the mark. Knowledge of the Word of God and Prayer are our weapons of offense, and Faith is our weapon of defense.

"If My people who are called by My name will humble themselves, and pray and seek My face, and turn from their wicked ways, then I will hear from heaven, and will forgive their sin and heal their land. Now My eyes will be open and My ears attentive to prayer made in this place." [10]

United Prayer is vital in this conflict, prayer looking to break through the enemy's strongholds, to rescue the lost souls of men, women, and children all over the earth. Fasting adds extra power to prayer. The shield of Faith and the rest of the Armor of God will help us stand our ground and protect us from the fiery darts of the enemy.

This is not the end; we continue this series in Volume 2, as we look even closer at, "Removing The Veil of this present age of darkness," and how we, "as Believers" have "the Victory" in the Lord Jesus Christ.

REFERENCE VERSES LIST

47 (Titus 1:1, 2)
48 (Ephesians 2:4-9)
49 (Philippians 4:3)
50 (Romans 10:9, 10)

Chapter 2 Outline of the Eternal Plan

1 (Job 42:2 MSG)
2 (Ephesians 3:14 NLT)
3 (Ephesians 1:11)
4 (Colossians 1:16, 17)
5 (Nehemiah 9:6; 1Corinthians 15:40)
6 (Genesis 1:26-28; 2:7)
7 (Galatians 5:22, 23)
8 (Ezekiel 28:11-19; Isaiah 14:12-21)
9 (Genesis 3)
10 (Romans 5:19)
11 (1Chronicles 29:11)
12 (Matthew 28:18-20; 1John 5:7)
13 (Genesis 1:28; 9:1)
14 (Isaiah 65:17, 66:22; 2Peter 3:13, Revelation 21:1)
15 (Romans 4:11; 5:9, 19)
16 (Revelation 5:9; 7:9)
17 (1John 3:24; 4:13)
18 (John 3:3-7)
19 (2Corinthians 5:1-5)
20 (Romans 8:15, 23; Ephesians 1:5)
21 (1Peter 2:9)
22 (2Peter 3:13)

Chapter 3 The Center of God's Incredible Plan

1 (Jeremiah 29:11-13 AMP)
2 (Joshua 24:15)
3 (Hebrews 3:7-15)
4 (Matthew 12:36; 1Peter 4:5; Romans 14:12)
5 (Revelation 22:17)
6 (1John 3:8)
7 (Isaiah 28:29)
8 (Ephesians 3:10)
9 (Hebrews 2:10)
10 (Philippians 2:9; Ephesians 1 20-22)

11 (Hebrews 9:27)
12 (Acts 10:36; 17:24)
13 (Ephesians 3:12)
14 (Hebrews 6:19)
15 (John 1:14)
16 (Philippians 2:6-11)
17 (Philippians 2:5)
18 (John 8:12)
19 (John 1:14)
20 (John 13:34, 35; 1John 4:9-11)
21 (John 3:16)
22 (John 15:13)
23 (Hebrews 9:27)
24 (2Corinthians 8:9)
25 (Galatians 1:4, 5; 2Corinthians 5:18, 19)
26 (Romans 4:1-8)
27 (Luke 22:44)
28 (Matthew 26:37-39)
29 (Matthew 26:47-50)
30 (Matthew 26:55)
31 (Mark 14:55-61)
32 (Luke 22:63-65)
33 (John 19:1-5)
34 (Luke 23:44-49)
35 (Hebrews 2:14; 1John 3:8)
36 (Isaiah 52:13; Philippians 2:9)
37 (Ephesians 2:1)
38 (Isaiah 42:7; Luke 4:18)
39 (Matthew 24:14)
40 (Hebrews 1:3)
41 (1Timothy 2:5)
42 (Philippians 2:9)
43 (Romans 5:15-19)
44 (John 19:30)
45 (Matthew 1:21)
46 (John 3:16)
47 (Ephesians 1:4 TLB)
48 (John 15:16, 17)

Part 2 The Sovereign One
Chapter 4 The Sovereign One

1 (Psalms 93:1, 2)
2 (Galatians 1:4 NLT)

3 (Isaiah 6:1-3)
4 (Isaiah 6:4, 5)
5 (Psalms 24:1 NLT)
6 (Psalms 50:11, 12)
7 (Psalms 89:11)
8 (Isaiah 46:10)
9 (Job 12:10)
10 (Jeremiah 10:10-12 NLT)
11 (Job 23:13, 14 NLT)
12 (Revelation 22:13)
13 (Isaiah 41:4 AMP)
14 (Deuteronomy 6:4, 5)
15 (1Kings 8:60)
16 (John 4:24)
17 (Psalms 104:27-30)
18 (John 3:16)
19 (Proverbs 6:16)
20 (Psalms 75:6)
21 (1Peter 5:6)
22 (Psalms 75:7)
23 (Zephaniah 3:17)
24 (Jeremiah 32:41)
25 (Genesis 6:6)
26 (Psalms 94:9, 10)
27 (1Peter 5:7)
28 (Isaiah 45:12)
29 (Daniel 4:35 NLT)
30 (Job 9:12 NLT)
31 (Psalms 135:6 NLT)
32 (Romans 9:15 NLT)
33 (Romans 9:19 NLT)
34 (Romans 9:20-24 NLT)
35 (Isaiah 44:25 NLT)
36 (Isaiah 40:23)
37 (Proverbs 21:1 NLT)
38 (Daniel 2:21 NLT)
39 (Psalms 75:7 NLT)
40 (Job 12:10)
41 (Job 12:10-25 AMP)
42 (Psalms 104:14-27)
43 (Genesis 8:22 NLT)
44 (Acts 14:17 NLT)
45 (Psalms 135:6, 7)
46 (Psalms 147:8)
47 (Psalms 147:16-18 NLT)

48 (Psalm 40:16)
49 (1Peter 2:9)
50 (Hosea 14:2 NLT)
51 (Psalm 148:1-14 AMP)
52 (Romans 11:36 AMP)
53 (Hebrews 13:15 AMP)
54 (Revelation 4:11 NLT)

Chapter 5 The Trinity – A closer look at God

1 (1John 5:7, 8)
2 (Genesis 1:26)
3 (Genesis 3:22)
4 (Genesis 11:7)
5 (Isaiah 6:8)
6 (John 14:9)
7 (John 6:38, 39 NLT)
8 (John 14:16)
9 (John 14:26)
10 (John 15:26)
11 (Isaiah 48:16)
12 (Zechariah 4:6)
13 (Ephesians 4:4-6)
14 (1Timothy 2:5)
15 (Ephesians 1:4-12 AMP)
16 (Ephesians 2:7 AMP)
17 (Ephesians 3:11 AMP)
18 (2Thessalonians 2:6-8)
19 (John 16:7)
20 (1John 2:1)
21 John 6:46 NLT)
22 (John 1:18)
23 (Colossians 1:15-18 NLT)
24 (Hebrews 1:3 AMP)
25 (Revelation 1:8)
26 (Micah 5:2)
27 (Exodus 3:2)
28 (John 1:1, 2)
29 (Genesis 1:3)
30 (Genesis 2:7)
31 (John 20:22).
32 (Genesis 2:8)
33 (Genesis 3:8-11)
34 (Genesis 3:13-15)

35 (Genesis 4:9)
36 (Genesis 6:14-17)
37 (Genesis 11:5-8)
38 (Genesis 12:1-7)
39 (Genesis 15:1-21; 17:1-27)
40 (Genesis 18:1-33)
41 (Genesis 32:24-32)
42 (Exodus 3:6)
43 (Exodus 3:13-15)
44 (Genesis 22:15-18)
45 (Joshua 24:5)
46 (John 1:29; 1Corinthians 5:7)
47 (Exodus 12:1-11)
48 (Exodus 12:21, 22)
49 (Exodus 12:8, 9)
50 (Exodus 12:46; John 19:36)
51 (Exodus 12:12, 13)
52 (Romans 5:9; Luke 22:19-20)
53 (Genesis 3:21)
54 (Genesis 4:3-5)
55 (Genesis 22:1-19)
56 (Hebrews 9:22; 1Peter 1:2)
57 (1John 1:7, 9)
58 (John 1:29)
59 (Revelation 13:8)
60 (Exodus 25:40)
61 (Joshua 5:13-15)
62 (Deuteronomy 18:15, 18)
63 (1Corinthians 15:45-49)
64 (John 1:14)
65 (Hebrews 10:5)
66 (John 14:1-6)
67 (Matthew 16:16)
68 (John 6:35, 41, 48, 51)
69 (John 8:12)
70 (John 10:7, 9)
71 (John 10:11, 14)
72 (John 11:25)
73 (John 14:6)
74 (John 15:1, 5)
75 (John 1:4)
76 (1Peter 1:20 NLT)
77 (Matthew 16:28-17:9)
78 (John 1:14 AMP)
79 (2Peter 1:16-18 NLT)

80 (1Peter 2:24 NLT)
81 (Matthew 28:19-20)
82 (John 14:16, 26; 15:26; 16:7)
83 (Genesis 11)
84 (Acts 2:5-39)
85 (Acts 2:41)
86 (Genesis 2:17)
87 (1Kings 19:18)
88 (1Thessalonians 5:8)
89 (John 16:11)
90 (Revelation 20:1, 2)
91 (Romans 3:23)
92 (John 16:12-15)

Chapter 6 Foreknowledge

1 (Romans 8:29)
2 (1Peter 1:1, 2)
3 (Isaiah 44:6-8 AMP)
4 (Isaiah 45:21)
5 (Ephesians 3:10)
6 (Revelation 21:27)
7 (John 15:16)
8 (Matthew 21:42)
9 (2Peter 3:9)
10 (Mark 8:35)
11 (Matthew 6:19, 20)
12 (John 14:1-3)
13 (Revelation 13:8; 17:8)
14 (Romans 8:28-30)
15 (Genesis 16:13)
16 (Hebrews 13:8)
17 (Isaiah 57:15)
18 (Isaiah 40:26)
19 (Isaiah 55:9)
20 (Proverb 20:27)
21 (1Samuel 16:7)
22 (2Chronicles 16:9)
23 (Matthew 7:21-23)
24 (Mark 11:24)
25 (Romans 4:3-5 AMP)
26 (Hebrews 13:5)
27 (Philippians 4:19)
28 (1Kings 19:11-13)
29 (Romans 8:1, 4; Galatians 5:16)

30 (Deuteronomy 7:9; Isaiah 30:18;
  1Corinthians 10:13)

Part 3 Knowing the Plan
Chapter 7 Rightly Dividing the Word

1 (2Timothy 2:15)
2 (Psalms 19:7-14 AMP)
3 (2Timothy 2:15 AMP)
4 (2Timothy 3:16, 17 AMP)
5 (1Corinthians 10:11)
6 (John 5:39)
7 (2Timothy 3:16, 17)
8 (1Corinthians 10:11)
9 (Romans 11:25)
10 (1Corinthians 10:11)
11 (1Corinthians 14:33)
12 (2Timothy 2:15)
13 (1Corinthians 3:8-15)
14 (John 14:1-4)
15 (Revelation 5:10)
16 (Galatians 6:10)

Chapter 8 The Purpose of the Plan

1 (Isaiah 14:26 NLT)
2 (2Peter 3:10-13)
3 (Ephesians 1:9, 10)
4 (Matthew 25 34-46)
5 (Isaiah 14:24 AMP)
6 (1John 3:8-10 AMP)
7 (Isaiah 46:10, 11)
8 (2Corinthians 5:18-21 NLT)
9 (Ephesians 3:9 NLT)
10 (Isaiah 45:18)
11 (Proverbs 16:4)
12 (Matthew 6:10)
13 (Romans 8:28)
14 (Romans 11:25)
15 (Isaiah 14:27 NLT)
16 (Jeremiah 51:29 NLT)
17 (Matthew 24:35)
18 (Isaiah 65:17)
19 (Romans 4:17)
20 (Romans 9:17)

21 (Exodus 9:16)
22 (Zechariah 4:6)
23 (1Corinthians 1:18-31)
24 (Romans 1:4; 6:4)
25 (2Peter 3:9)
26 (Ephesians 1:9)
27 (Philippians 3:10)
28 (Romans 8:1, 4; Galatians 5:16)
29 (1John 3:8)
30 (Matthew 21:33-39 NIV)
31 (John 8:44 AMP)
32 (1Corinthians 2:6-8)

Part 4 Light from the Prophetic Word
Chapter 9 Prophecy: The Plan Given

1 (Ephesians 4:15, Colossians 1:18)
2 (2Peter 1:19-21 NLT)
3 Isaiah 55:10, 11 NLT)
4 (Hebrews 1:1 AMP)
5 (Revelation 19:10)
6 (Luke 24:44)
7 (Matthew 24:27, 30, 37, 39, 44)
8 (Revelation 3:14)
9 (Acts 3:15)
10 (Hebrews 5:9)
11 (Hebrews 12:2)
12 (Matthew 5:17 AMP)
13 (Matthew 5:18 AMP)
14 (John 20:28)
15 (Amos 3:7, 8)
16 (Hosea 12:10)
17 (Hosea 12:13)
18 (2Peter 1:19)
19 (Daniel 2:31-45)
20 (Isaiah 7:14; 9:6, 7; 11:1-3)
21 (Acts 2:32, 3:15; 4:10)
22 (Acts 2:1-4)
23 (Luke 21:20-24)
24 (1Thessalonians 5:1-5)
25 (2Corinthians 5:10)
26 (2Thessalonians 2:3)
27 (Matthew 24:21; Revelation 7:14)
28 (Jeremiah 30:7; Daniel 12:1)
29 (Revelation 13)

30 (Revelation 17-18)

31 (Zechariah 14:1-3; Revelation 19:17-21)

32 (Revelation 19:17-21; Zechariah 14:4-11; Malachi 3:1-3; 4:1-6)

33 (Matthew 25:31-46)

34 (Revelation 20:1-3)

35 (Revelation 20:4-6)

36 (Revelation 20:7-10)

37 (2 Peter 3:5-13)

38 (Revelations 20:11-15)

39 (Isaiah 60:18-22; 65:17; Revelation 21:1-22:5)

40 (2Corinthians 4:3, 4)

41 (Matthew 24:4-14)

42 (2Thessalonians 2:11)

43 (John 5:39 AMP)

44 (John 14:26 NLT)

45 (John 16:13)

46 (1Peter 1:10-13 NLT)

47 (1Peter 1:10-13 MSG)

48 (Luke 10:18-24 NLT)

49 (Romans 15:4)

50 (Romans 16:25, 26 NLT)

Chapter 10 The Plan Unveiled

1 (2Corinthians 4:3-4 AMP)

2 (Hosea 4:6)

3 (John 16:15 AMP)

4 (1 Corinthians 2:16)

5 (2Corinthians 10:5, 6)

6 (2Timothy 3:16, 17 AMP)

7 (1Corinthians 2:14)

8 (John 15:26 AMP)

9 (Deuteronomy 29:29)

10 (John 16:13)

11 (Romans 8:16)

Chapter 11 The Plan Understood

1 (John 5:39 AMP)

2 (Luke 7:30 NLT)

3 (John 7:52 NLT)

4 (2 Peter 3:9)

5 (Matthew 21:28-32 NLT)

6 (1Timothy 6:10)

7 (1Corinthians 13:11)

8 (Hebrews 9:27)

9 (Acts 17:11)

10 (John 8:31, 32 NLT)

11 (Romans 12:2 NLT)

12 (Hebrews 11:6 AMP)

13 (John 5:39 MSG)

14 (2Corinthians 10:4)

15 (Philippians 4:8)

16 (Romans 10:8-15)

17 (2Corinthians 3:18)

18 (3John 1:2)

19 (Matthew 4:4 AMP)

20 (Hebrews 11:6)

21 (Colossians 3:16)

Part 5 Seeing the Plan

Chapter 12 A Book in Heaven

1 (Genesis 1:26)

2 (John 4:24)

3 (Exodus 20:4-6)

4 (Genesis 2:19, 20)

5 (Genesis 1:26-28)

6 (Acts 17:26)

7 (Psalms 139:1-6)

8 (Proverbs 5:21 MSG)

9 (Proverbs 22:12 AMP)

10 (Psalms 139:7-12)

11 (Proverbs 15:3)

12 (1Peter 3:12 NLT)

13 (Hebrews 4:13)

14 (Psalms 139:13-18)

15 (Job 10:10 NLT)

16 (Jeremiah 1:5)

17 (Galatians 1:15, 16 NLT)

18 (Psalms 34:15)

19 (Psalm 127:3)

20 (Luke 22:31, 32)

21 (Job 1:6-12; 2:1-7)

22 (Matthew 25:40)

23 (1John 2:15-17)

24 (Hebrews 5:14)

25 (2Corinthians 3:1-3)

26 (Ephesians 6:16)
27 (Hebrews 12:15)
28 (Ephesians 4:14, 15)
29 (Matthew 18:21-35 NLT)
30 (1Peter 4:8 AMP)
31 (2Corinthians 10:3-6)
32 (Job 13:15)
33 (Genesis 50:20)
34 (Romans 12:19)
35 (1Peter 2:9)
36 (Romans 8:16, 17)
37 (Hebrews 2:5-18)
38 (Hebrews 2:18 AMP)
39 (Psalms 56:8 NLT)
40 (Psalms 27:10 NLT)
41 (Matthew 12:46-50 NLT)
42 (Matthew 10:34-39 NLT)
43 (Revelation 13:8)
44 (Romans 1:20 NLT)
45 (Ephesians 2:10 AMP)
46 (2Timothy 3:16, 17)
47 (Philippians 1:6 AMP)
48 (Hebrews 13:5)
49 (Psalms 37:25)
50 (Proverbs 3:5, 6)
51 (Hebrews 13:5, 6 AMP)
52 (Isaiah 30:18 AMP)
53 (Isaiah 40:31)

Chapter 13 This Journey called Life.

1 (Philippians 3:14, 15)
2 (John 14:6)
3 (John 12:26)
4 (1Corinthians 10:12)
5 (1Corinthians 15:45-58 NLT)
6 (Ephesians 1:15-23 NLT)
7 (Revelation 3:17, 18)
8 (John 3:1-7)
9 (Ecclesiastes 12:6-8)

Chapter 14 Lord, Open our Eyes.

1 (Luke 11:34)
2 (Luke 24:27; 31, 32)
3 (Romans 8:3)

4 (Luke 4:6, 7)
5 (Revelation 11:15)
6 (1John 2:16)
7 (Luke 4:14-21; Isaiah 61:1, 2)
8 (Luke 8:43-48 NLT)
9 (Isaiah 42:7)
10 (Isaiah 29:18)
11 (Isaiah 35:5)
12 (Mark 5:1-20)
15 (Matthew 11:5)
14 (Matthew 24:15-35)
15 (Zechariah 12:10-14)
16 (1John 5:20)
17 (John 9:1-41 NIV)
18 (Acts 9:1-22 NIV)
19 (Acts 13:9)
20 Acts 26:12-18
21 (Galatians 1:16 AMP)
22 (Job 33:14-30 NLT)
Part 6 "Intelligent Designs"

Chapter 15 Intelligent Designs

1 (Jeremiah 32:17)
2 (Psalms 53:1)
3 (Romans 1:18-20)
4 (Proverbs 1:16-18)
5 (Romans 1:18-32 MSG)
6 (Isaiah 5:20)
7 (Proverbs 15:3 AMP)
8 (Proverbs 1:7)
9 (Isaiah 29:16)
10 (2Timothy 3:7)

Chapter 16 Genome Coding: By Design

1 (Genesis 1:24, 25)
2 (Genesis 6:20)
3 (Romans 12:4-8)
4 (1Corinthians 12:12-14)
5 (Matthew 4:43)
16 (Genesis 9:4; Leviticus 17:11, 14)

Chapter 17 Two Seed

1 (Mark 8:35-37 AMP)
2 (John 16:33)
3 (John 15:5)
4 (John 6:63)
5 (Galatians 6:8)
6 (1Corinthians 15:35-38)
7 (John 12:23-25 NLT)
8 (John 4:36)
9 (Luke 16:8)
10 (Genesis 3:19 AMP)
11 (Job 34:15 AMP)
12 (Ecclesiastes 3:20)
13 (Ecclesiastes 12:7 AMP)
14 (Romans 5:12-21 NLT)
15 (Romans 8:10-13)
16 (John 12:26)

6 (Job 12:23 NLT)
7 (Matthew 5:13)
8 (Exodus 17:8-13)
9 (2Corinthians 10:3-5)
10 (2Chronicles 7:14, 15)

Translations used in Book.
New King James Version (NKJV)
New Living Translation (NLT)
King James Version (KJV)
Amplified Bible (AMP)
The Message (MSG)
The Living Bible (TLB)
Expanded Translation (ET)
New International Version (NIV)

Chapter 18 Two Views

1 (1Corinthians 15:33 NLT)
2 (Isaiah 5:20)
3 (Isaiah 29:14; 1Corinthians 1:19)
4 (Matthew 13:24-30)
5 (Matthew 13:36-43)